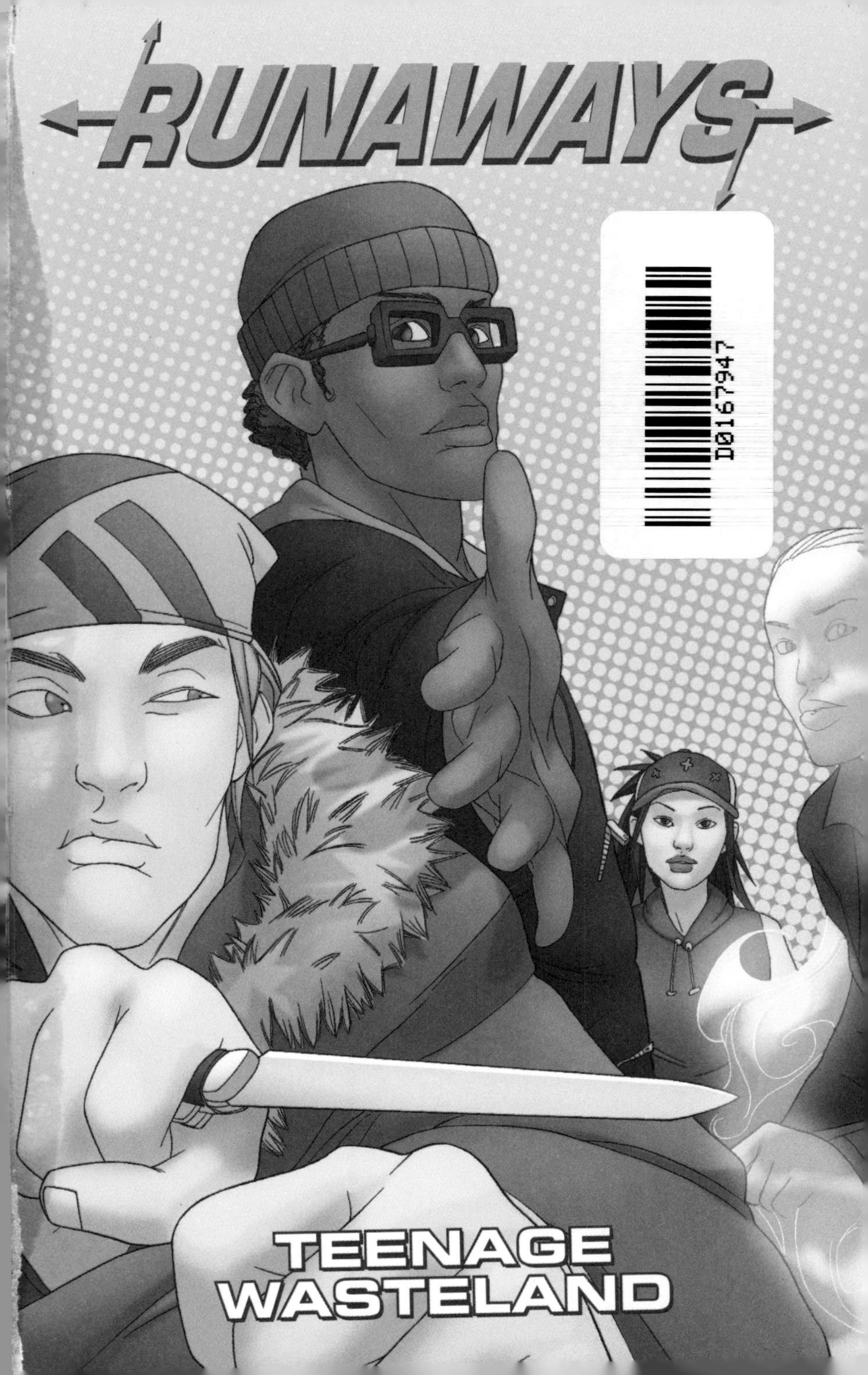
RUNAWAYS
TEENAGE
WASTELAND

RUNAWAYS

WRITER BRIAN K. VAUGHAN

PENCILS ADRIAN ALPHONA & TAKESHI MIYAZAWA (ISSUES #11-12)

INKS CRAIG YEUNG & DAVID NEWBOLD (ISSUES #11-12)

COLORS BRIAN REBER (ISSUES #7 & #11-12) & CHRISTINA STRAIN (ISSUES #8-10)

COVER ARTISTS JO CHEN & JOSH MIDDLETON (ISSUES #11-12)

LETTERS RANDY GENTILE WITH CHRIS ELIOPOULOS (ISSUE #10)

ASSISTANT EDITOR MACKENZIE CADENHEAD EDITOR C.B. CEBULSKI

RUNAWAYS CREATED BY BRIAN K. VAUGHAN & ADRIAN ALPHONA

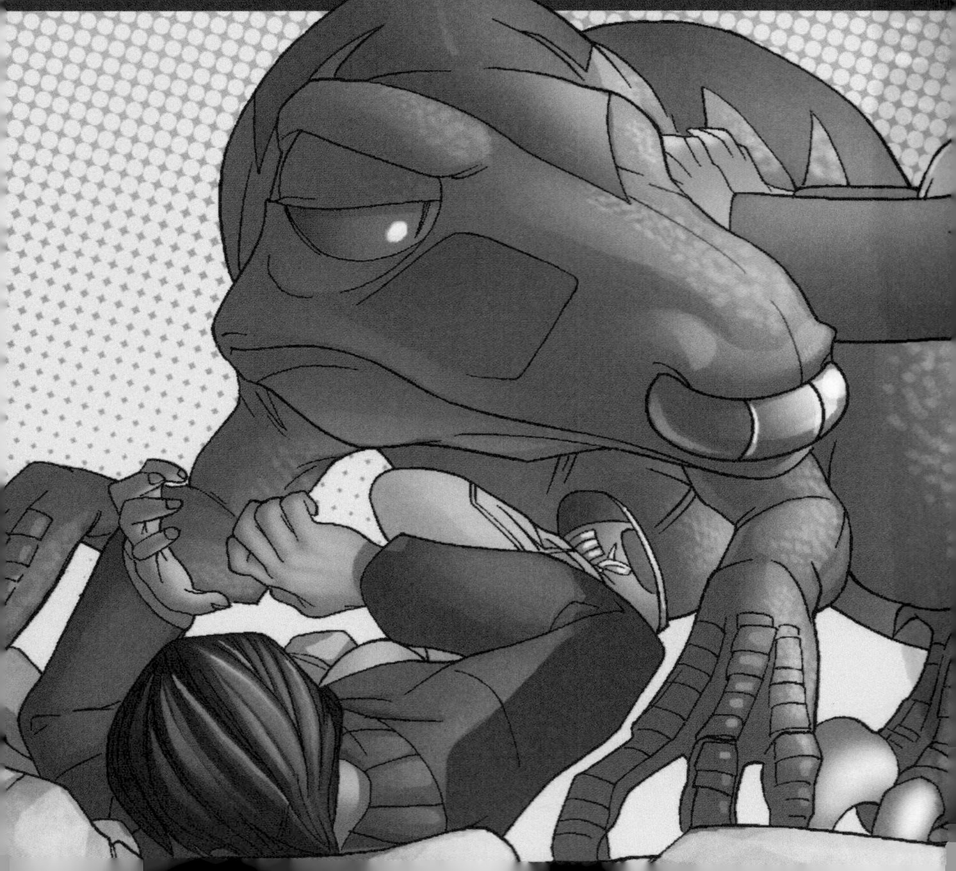

Collection Editor: Jennifer Grünwald
Editorial Assistants: James Emmett & Joe Hochstein
Assistant Editors: Alex Starbuck & Nelson Ribeiro
Editor, Special Projects: Mark D. Beazley
Senior Editor, Special Projects: Jeff Youngquist
Vice President of Sales: David Gabriel
Book Design: Jeff Powell

Editor in Chief: Axel Alonso
Chief Creative Officer: Joe Quesada
Publisher: Dan Buckley
Executive Producer: Alan Fine

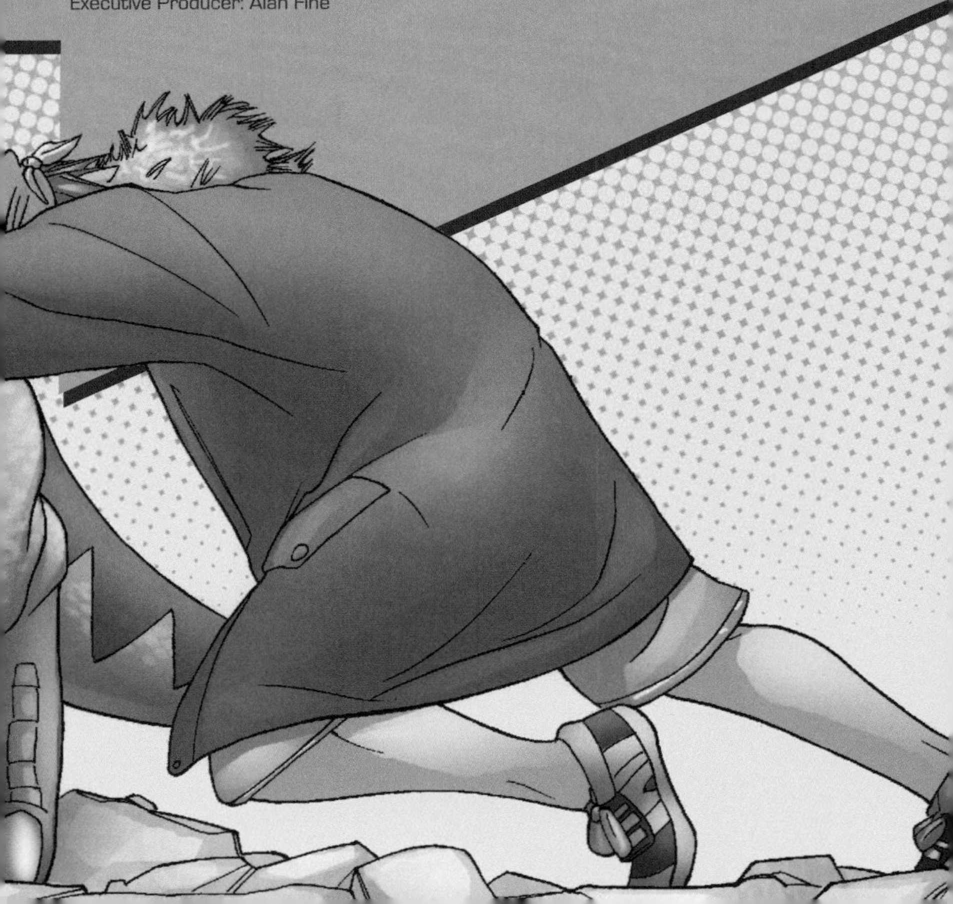

KAROLINA DEAN

ALEX WILDER

MOLLY HAYES

Teenager Alex Wilder and five other only children always thought that their parents were boring Los Angeles socialites, until the kids witness the adults murder a young girl in some kind of dark sacrificial ritual. The teens soon learn that their parents are part of a secret organization called The Pride, a collection of crime bosses, time-travelling despots, alien overlords, mad scientists, evil mutants and dark wizards.

After stealing weapons and resources from these villainous adults (including a mystical staff, futuristic gauntlets and a genetically engineered velociraptor named Old Lace), the kids run away from home and vow to bring their parents to justice. But when the members of The Pride frame their children for the murder they committed, the fugitive Runaways are forced to retreat to a subterranean hideout nicknamed the Hostel. Using the diverse powers and skills they inherited, the Runaways now hope to atone for their parents' crimes by helping those in need.

NICO MINORU

GERTRUDE YORKES

CHASE STEIN

7

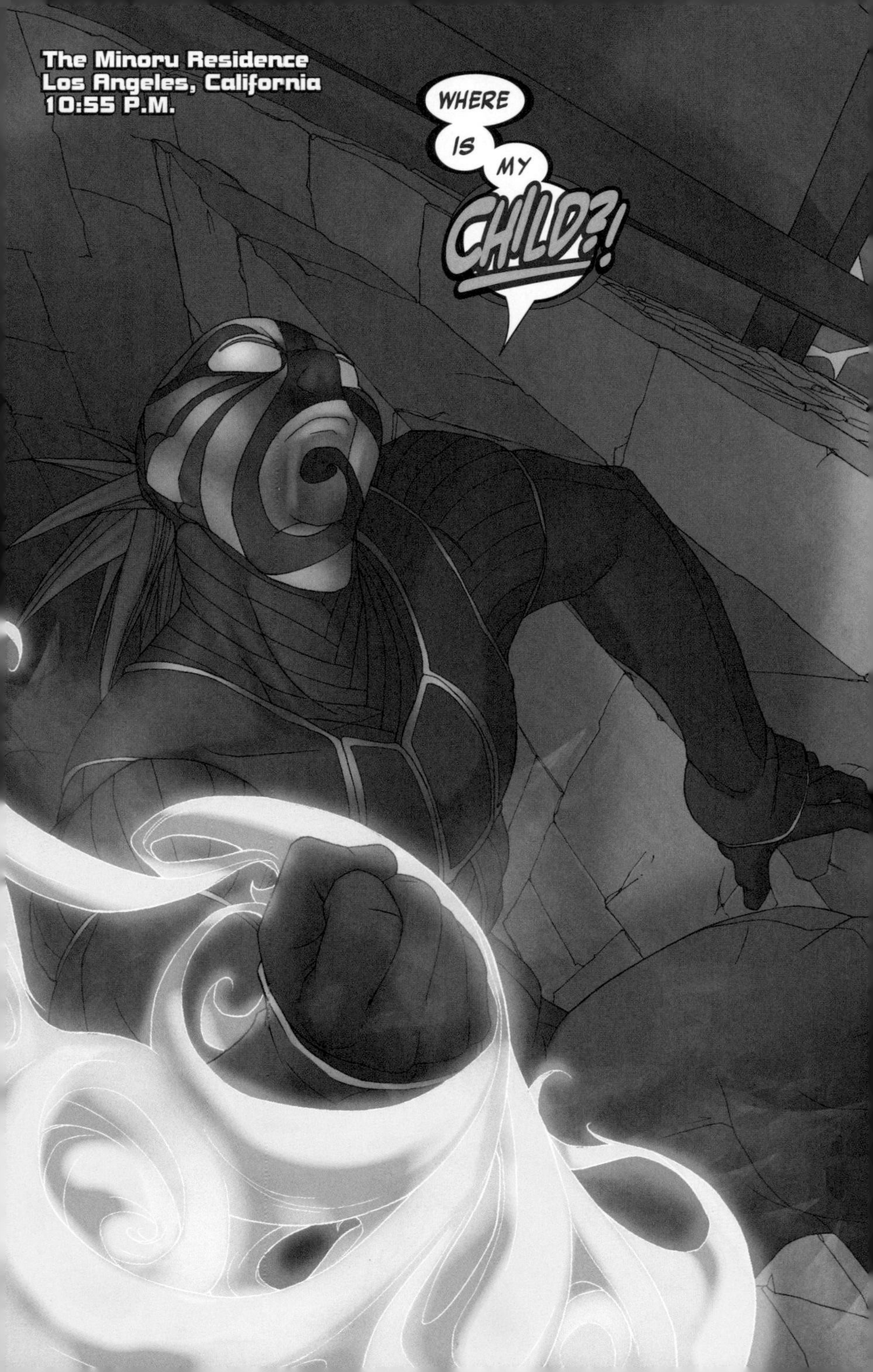
The Minoru Residence
Los Angeles, California
10:55 P.M.
WHERE IS MY CHILD?!

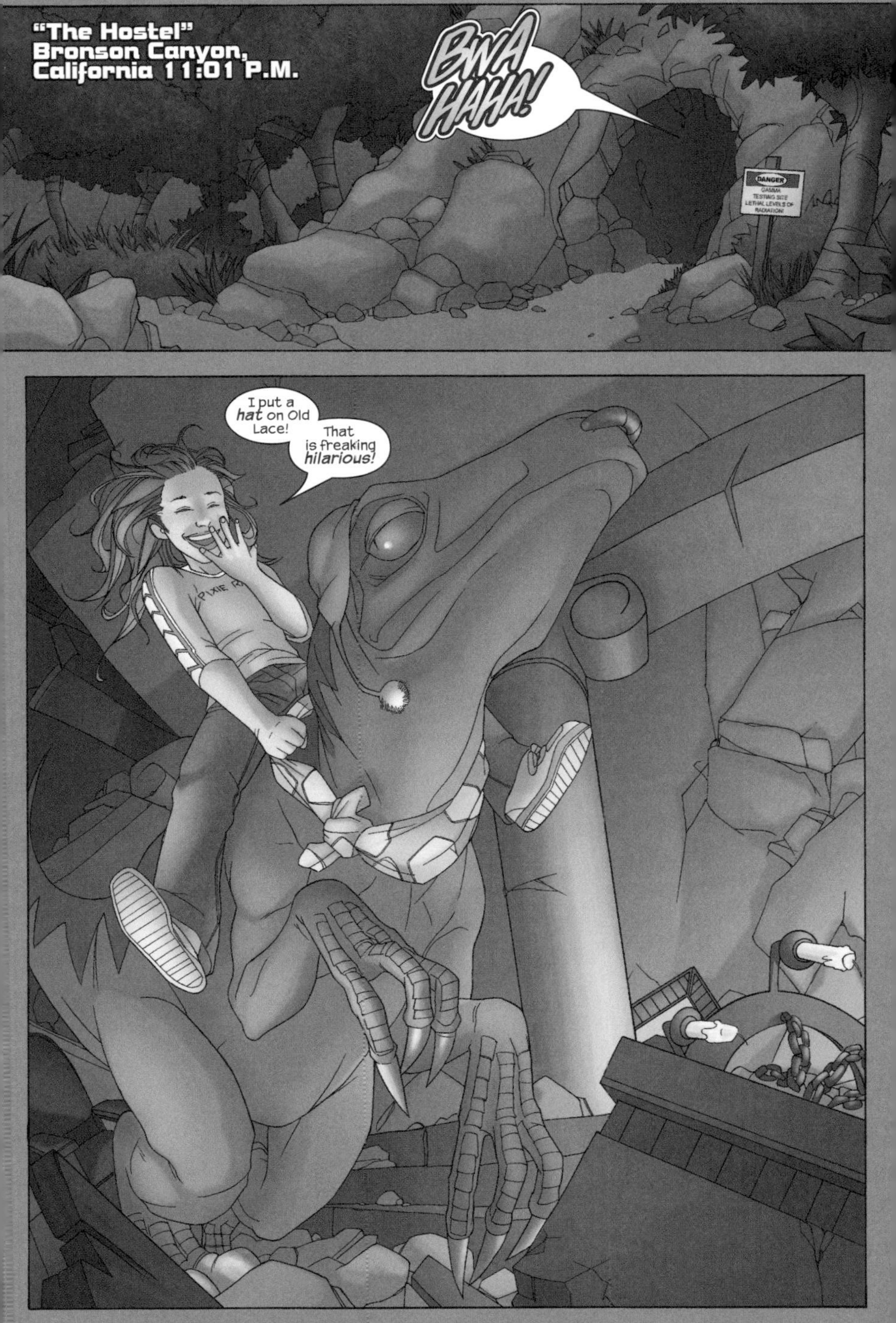
"The Hostel"
Bronson Canyon, California 11:01 P.M.
BWA HAHA!
DANGER
GAMMA TESTING SITE LETHAL LEVELS OF RADIATION!
I put a *hat* on Old Lace!
That is freaking *hilarious!*

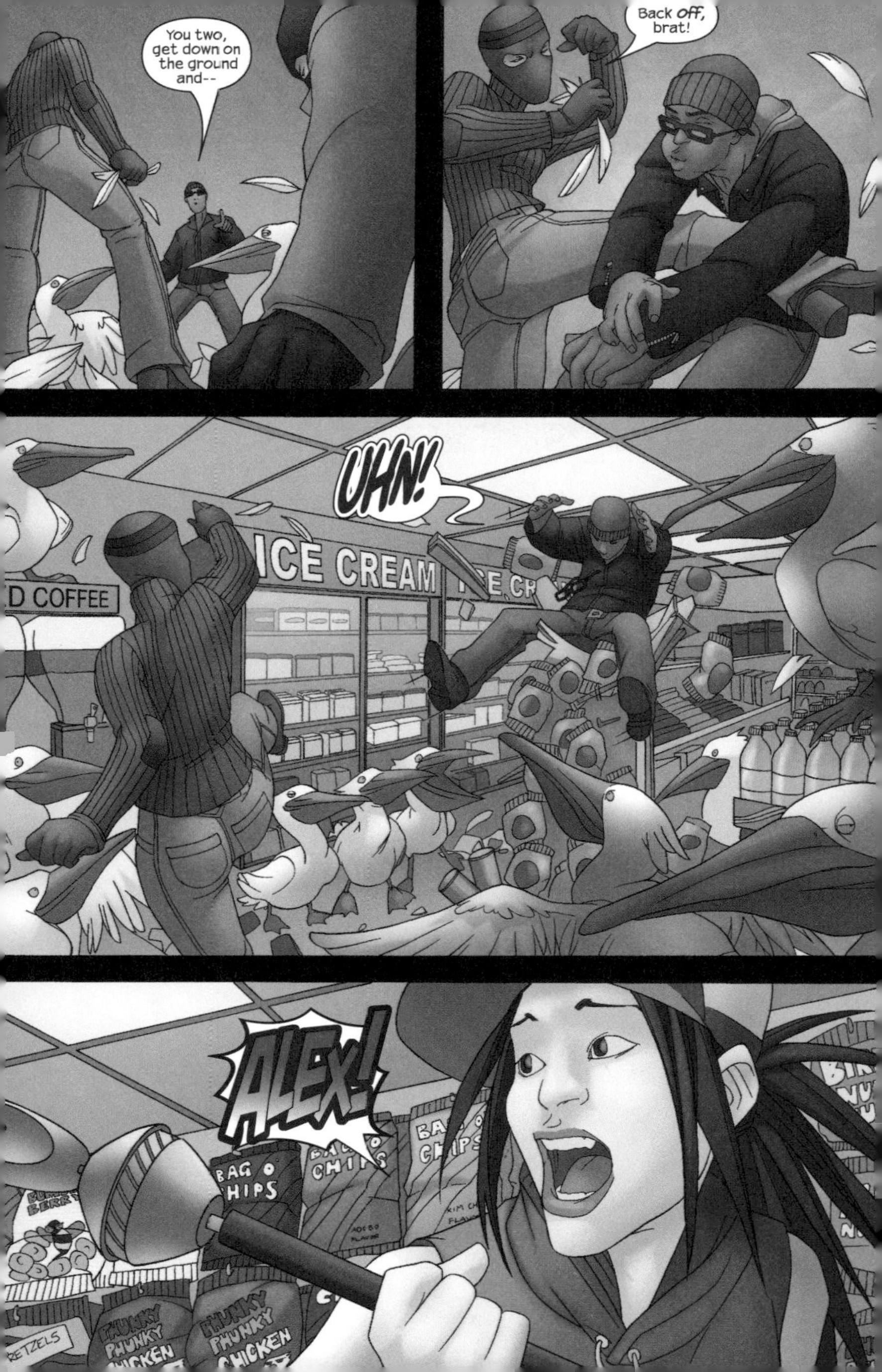

You two, get down on the ground and--
Back off, brat!
UHN!
ICE CREAM
D COFFEE
ALEX!
BAG O CHIPS
PHUNKY PHUNKY CHICKEN

Yeah, these jerk-holes must be mutants, or *cyborgs*, or...

Wha...?

Wow.

That's what *I* was about to say.

Please! Don't hurt me!

I... I never wanted to be a part of this! My mom and dad threatened to *kill* me if I didn't help them! You have to believe me. My parents are *evil*.

Cola

Cola

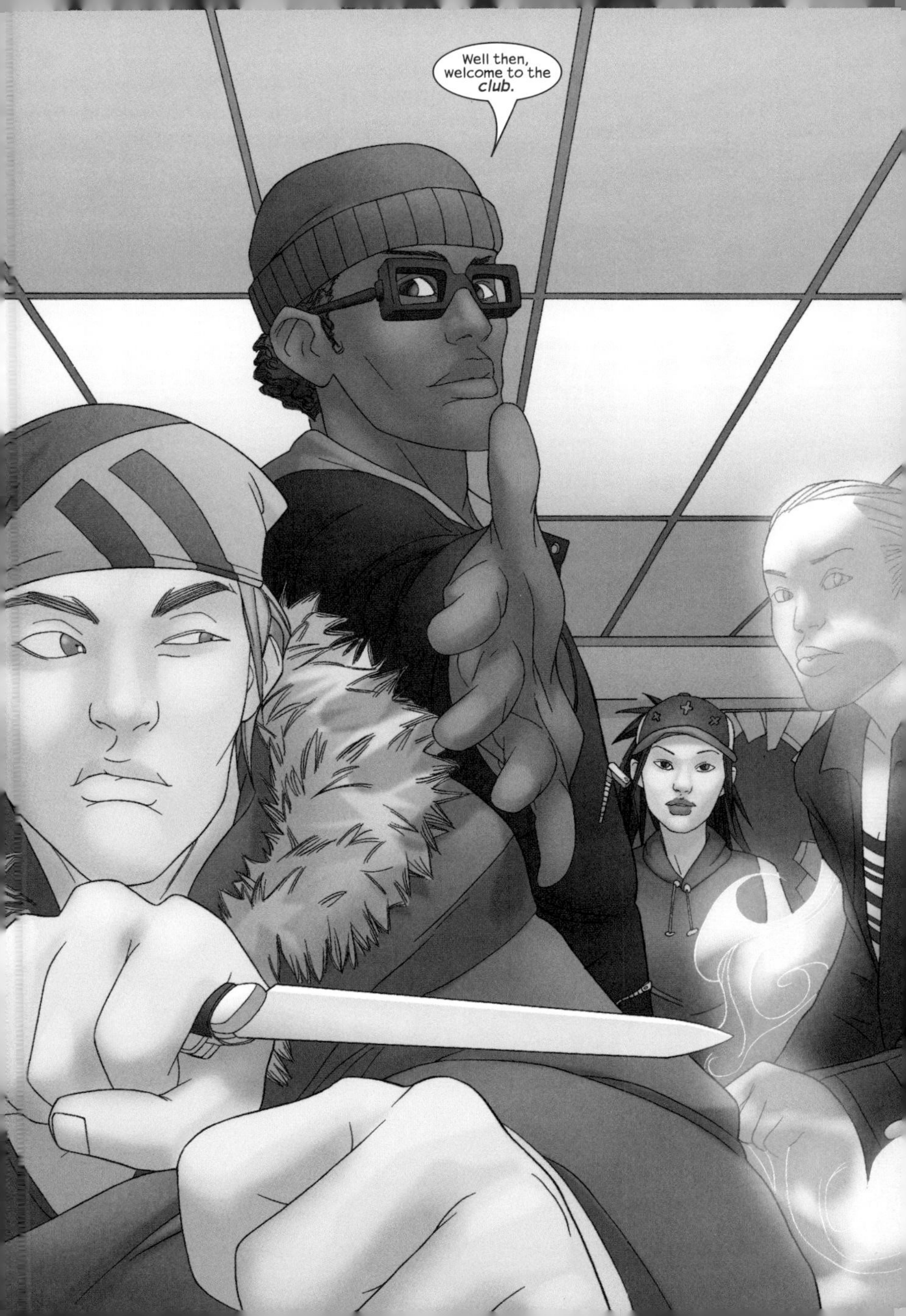
Well then, welcome to the *club.*

8

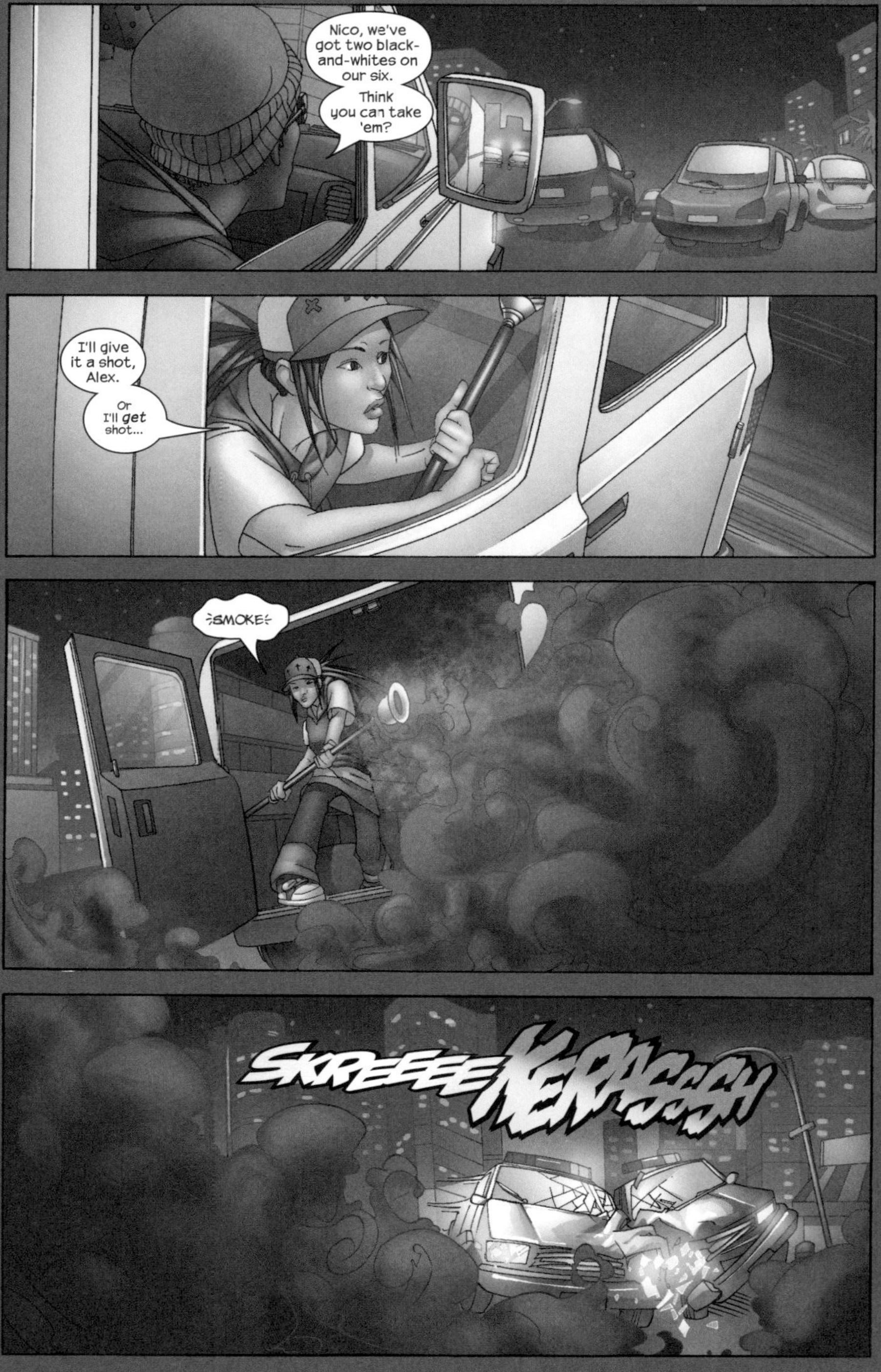
Nico, we've got two black-and-whites on our six.
Think you can take 'em?
I'll give it a shot, Alex.
Or I'll *get* shot...
SMOKE
SKREEEEE KERASSSH

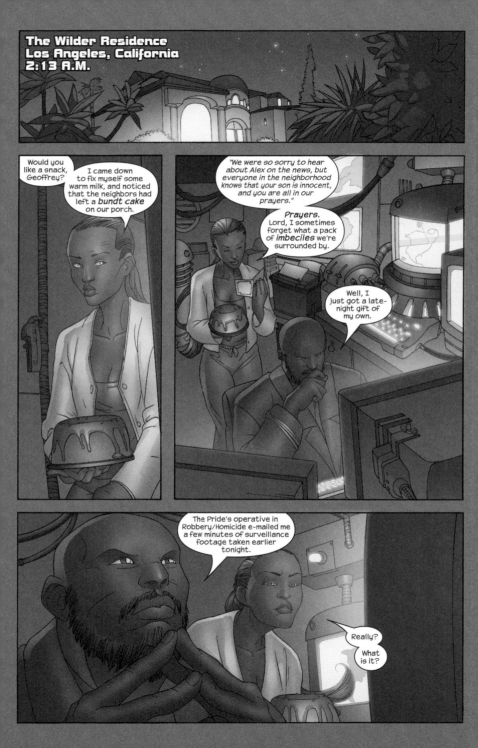

The Wilder Residence
Los Angeles, California
2:13 A.M.

Man, I don't know how you guys have adjusted so quickly to the fact that your parents are... you know.

We've had more time than you, Topher. It never really sinks in all the way, but it *will* start to feel like less of a bad dream.

It's like, growing up in Cali, you hear about Doc Ock and Venom and the Punisher and whatever on TV, but they always felt far away and... and *make-believe*.

Besides, unlike my folks, your mom and dad don't sound like they *chose* the path they're on. I'm sure we'll be able to get them some help. Set them straight again.

I hope so.

Ever since I was twelve, all I wanted was to get away from my stupid parents... and as soon as I get my wish, I just want everything back the way it was.

That's life, isn't it?

Yeah.

Yeah, I guess it is.

Topher, *wait.*

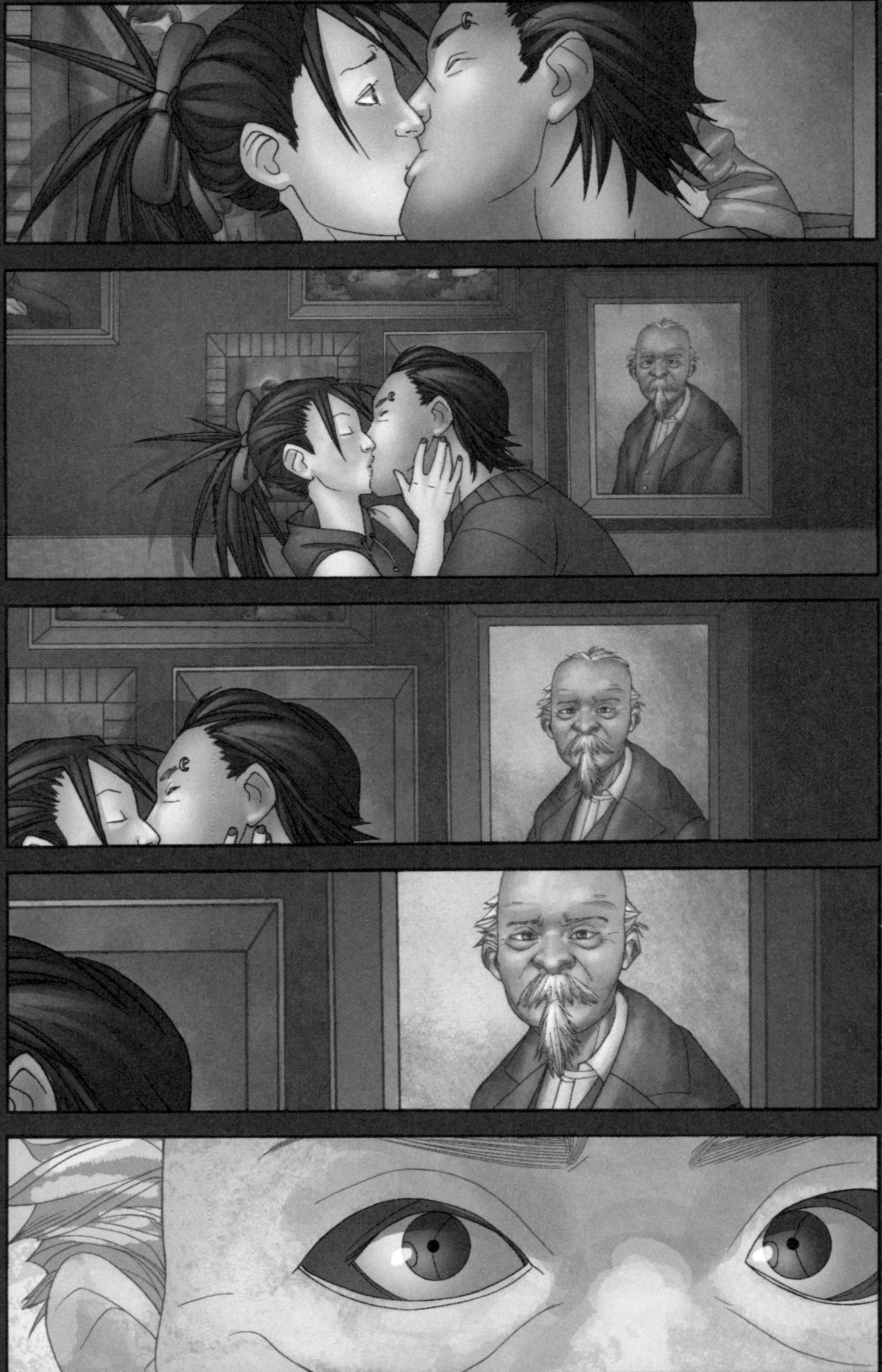

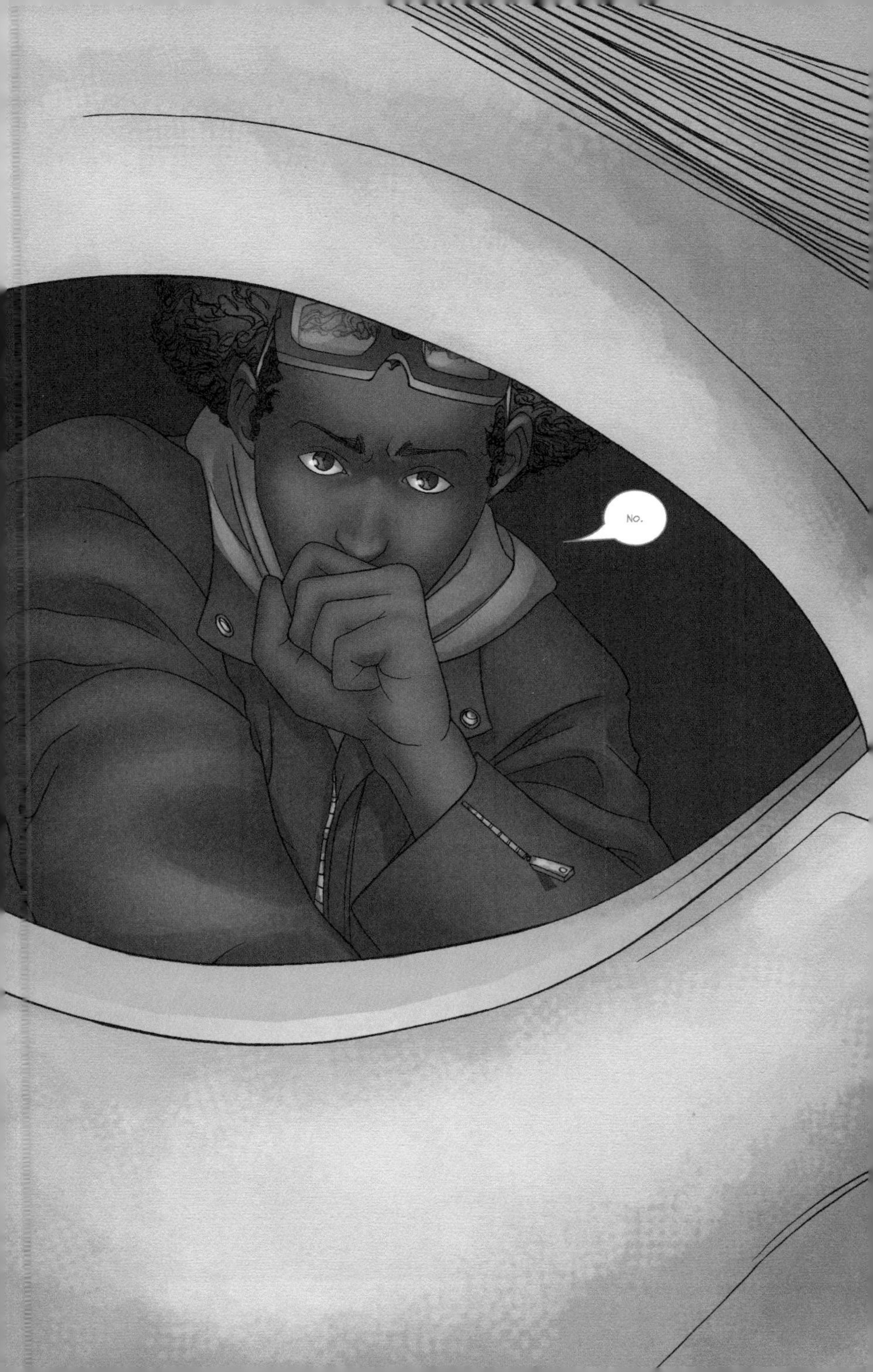
NO.

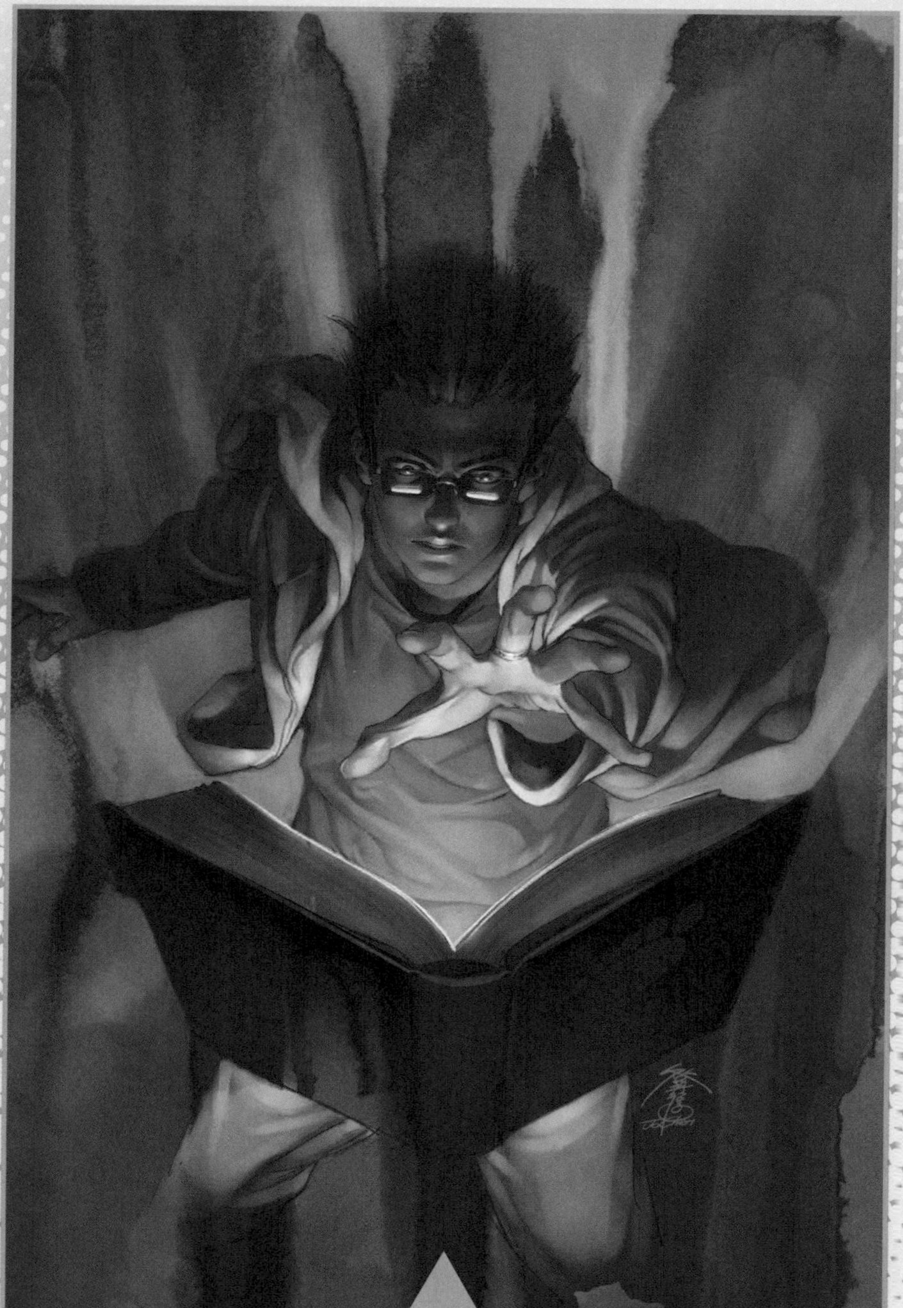

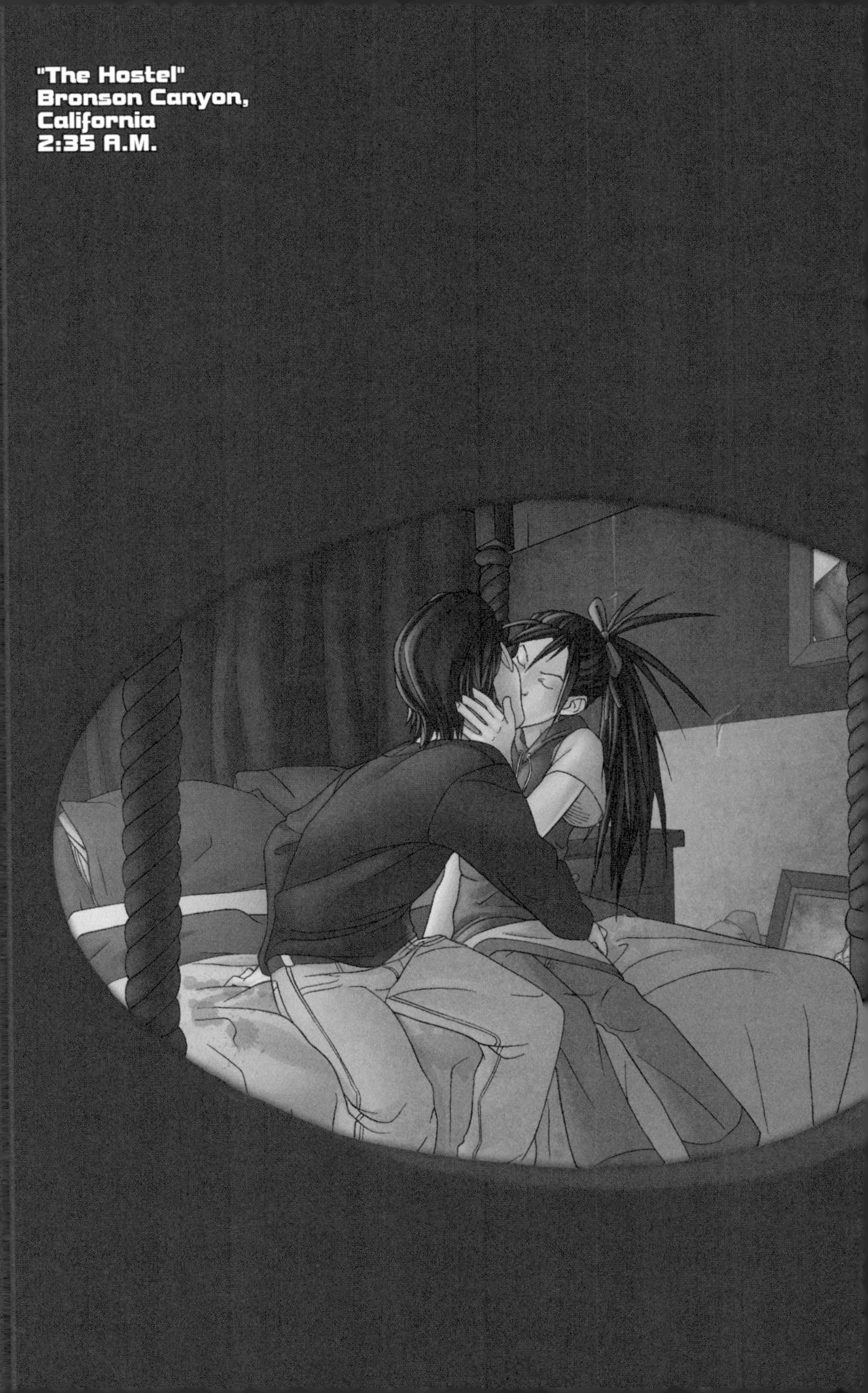
"The Hostel"
Bronson Canyon,
California
2:35 A.M.

DANGER
GAMMA
TESTING SITE
LETHAL LEVELS OF
RADIATION!

I don't know what to say, Alex.

You've been so sweet to me, and I've been acting like a total--

Nico...

No, you have to hear this.

I just did something completely awful, and you deserve to--

Nico, I already know that you and Topher kissed.

You... you do?

HOW?

Oh, our first night in the Hostel, I found this *secret room* next door. It's sorta like those passageways in my parents'--

You've been *spying* on me?

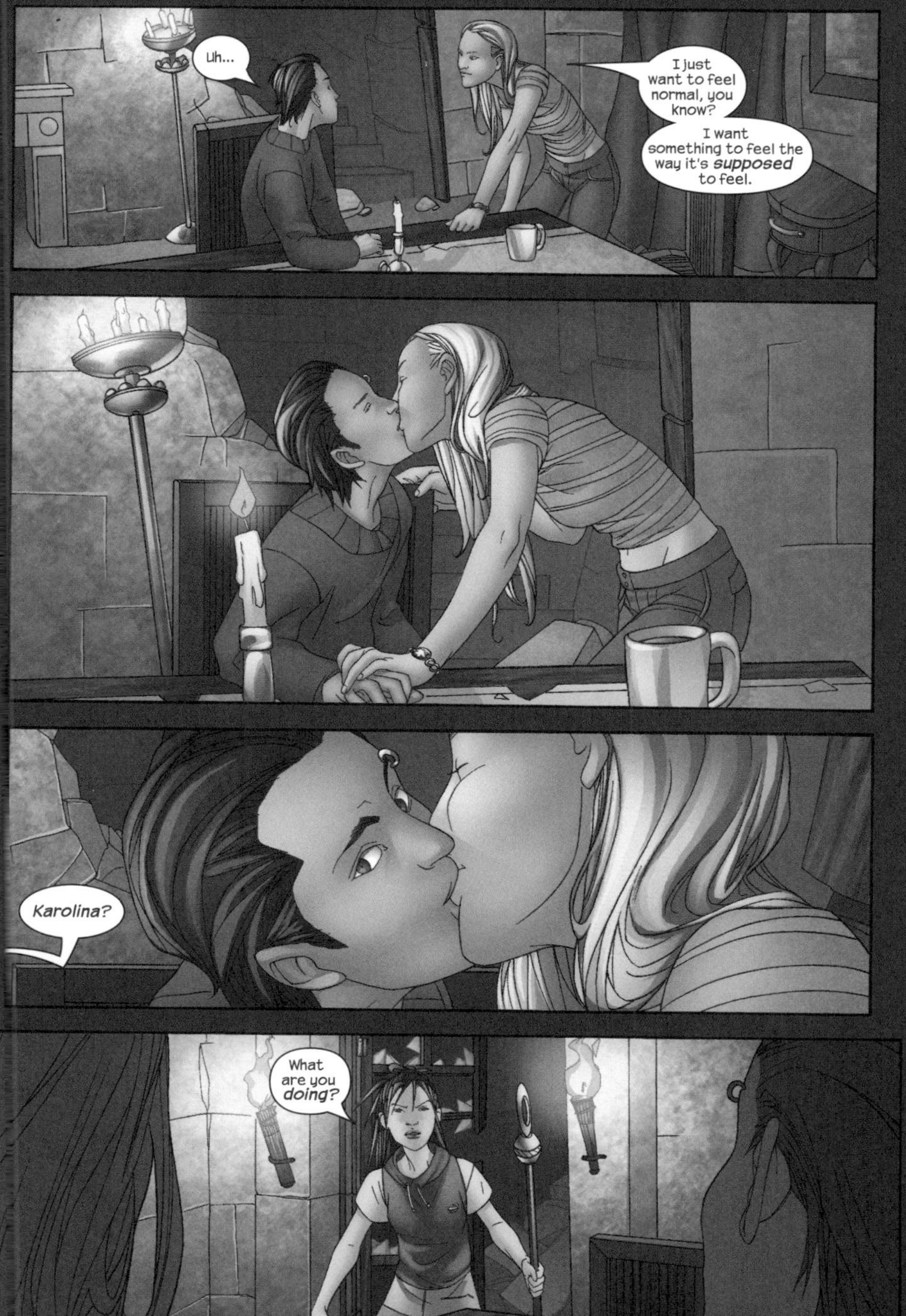
Uh...
I just want to feel normal, you know?
I want something to feel the way it's *supposed* to feel.
Karolina?
What are you *doing*?

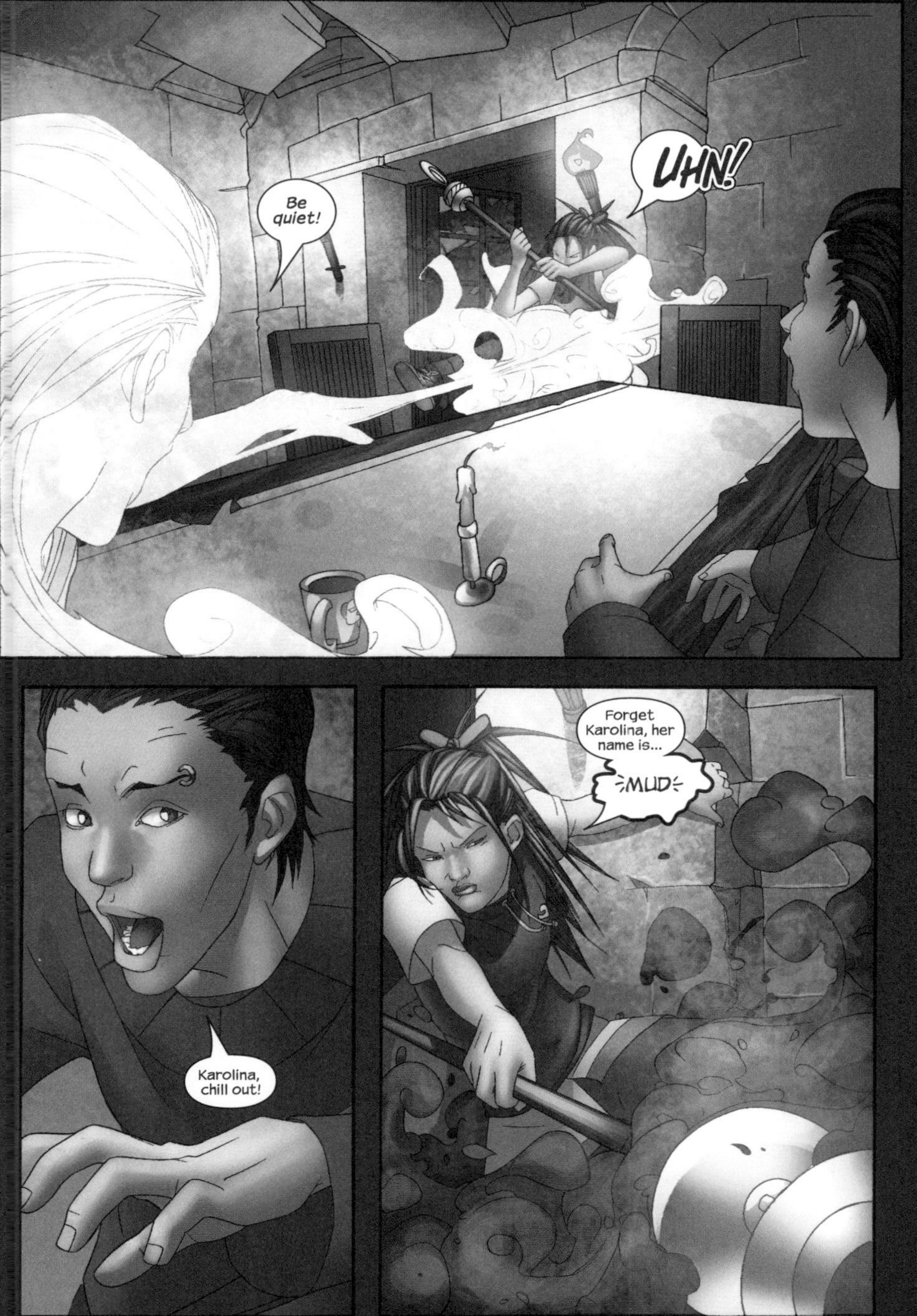
Be quiet!
UHN!
Karolina, chill out!
Forget Karolina, her name is...
MUD

10

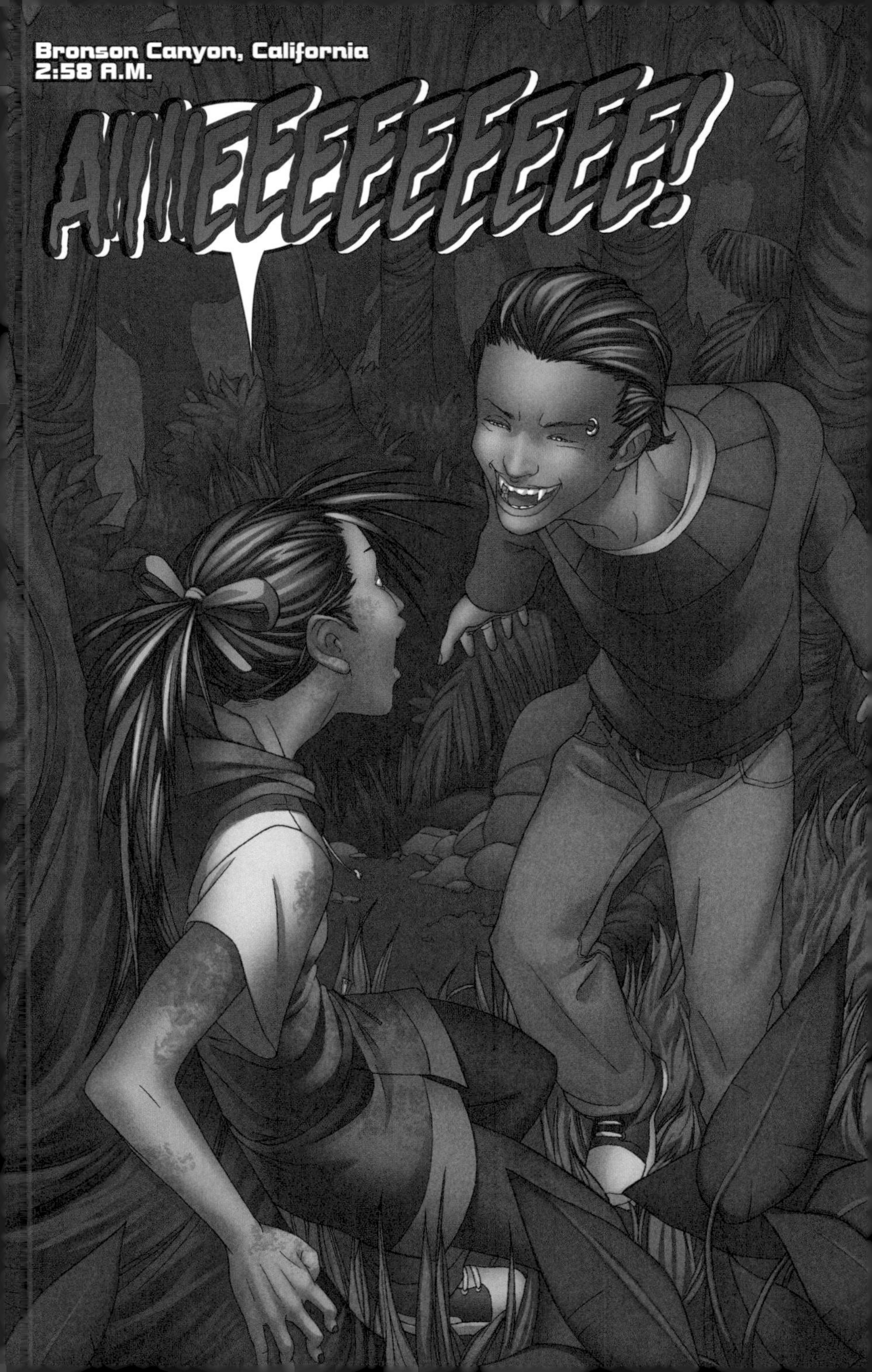
Bronson Canyon, California
2:58 A.M.
AIIIEEEEEEEEEEE!

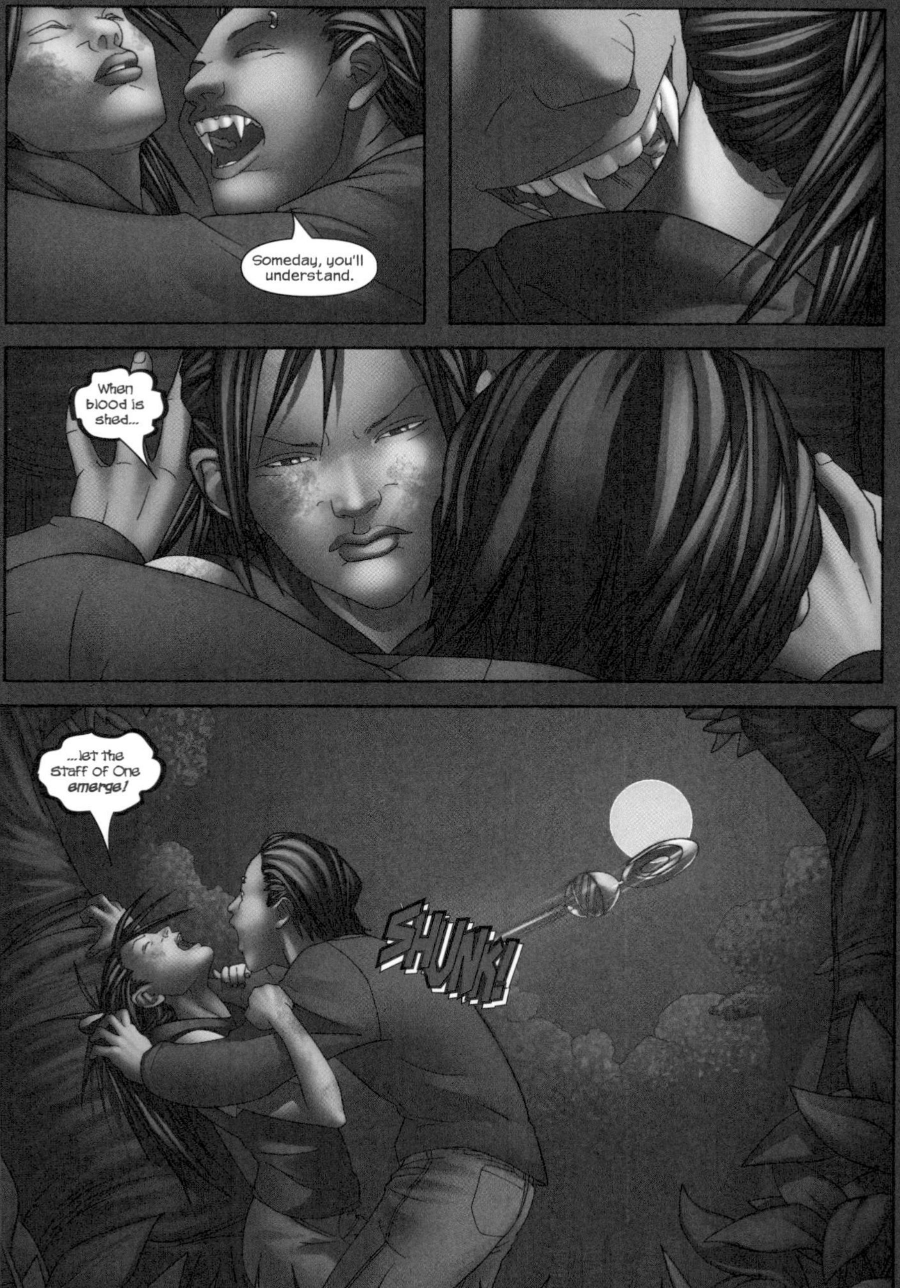

Someday, you'll understand.
When blood is shed...
...let the Staff of One *emerge!*
SHUNK!

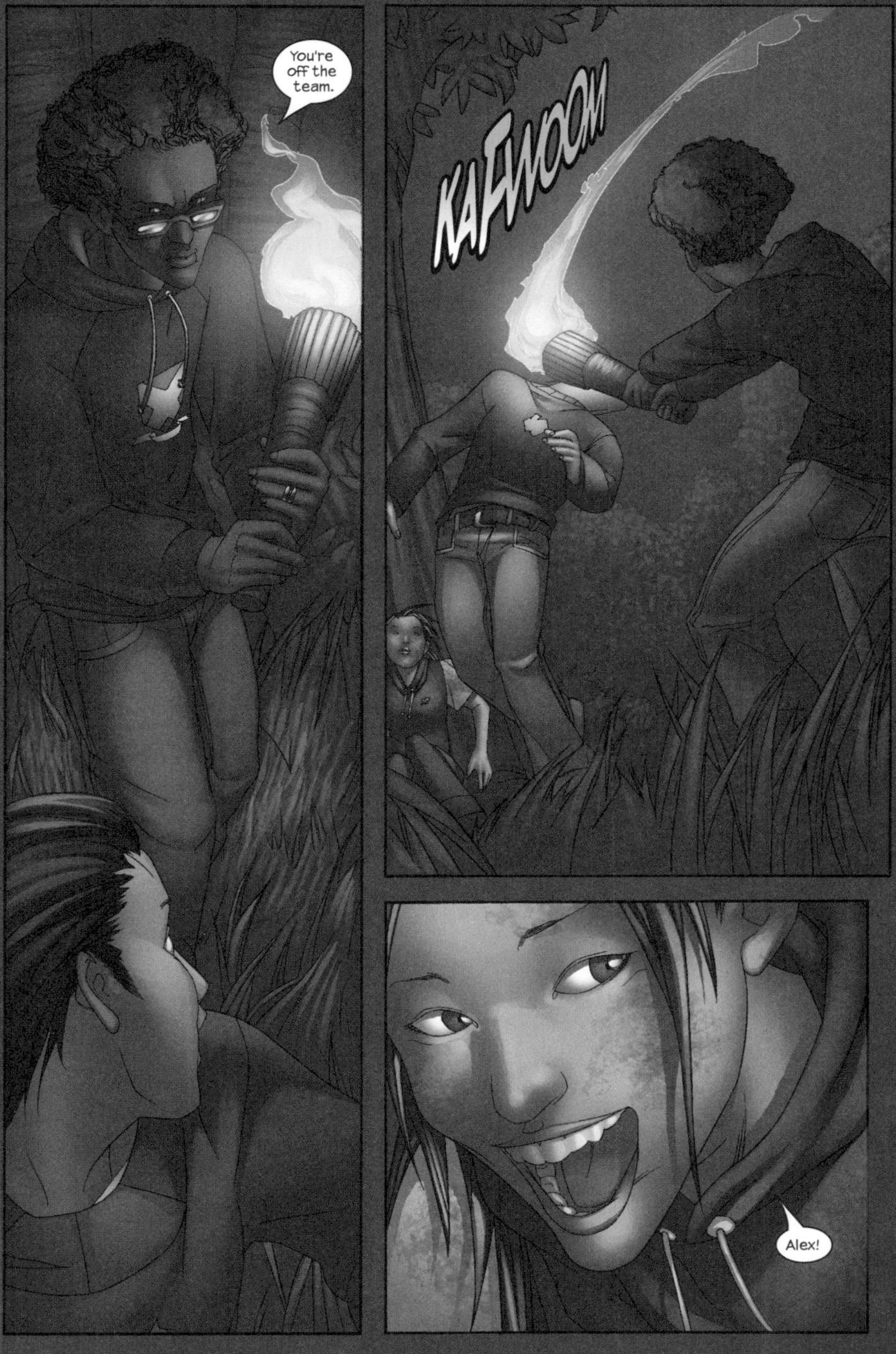
You're off the team.
KAFWOOM
Alex!

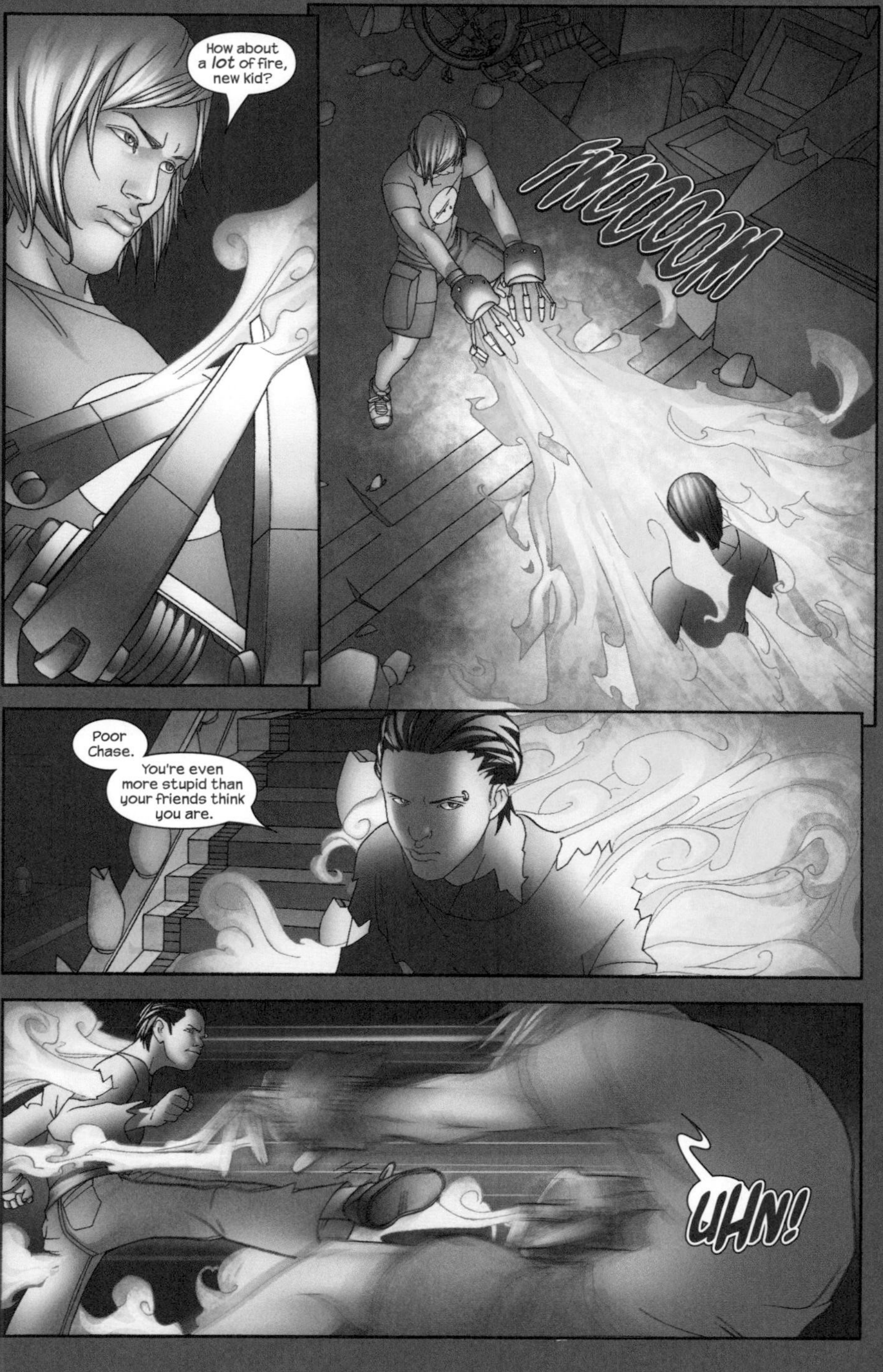
How about a *lot* of fire, new kid?
FWOOOOM
Poor Chase.
You're even more stupid than your friends think you are.
UHN!

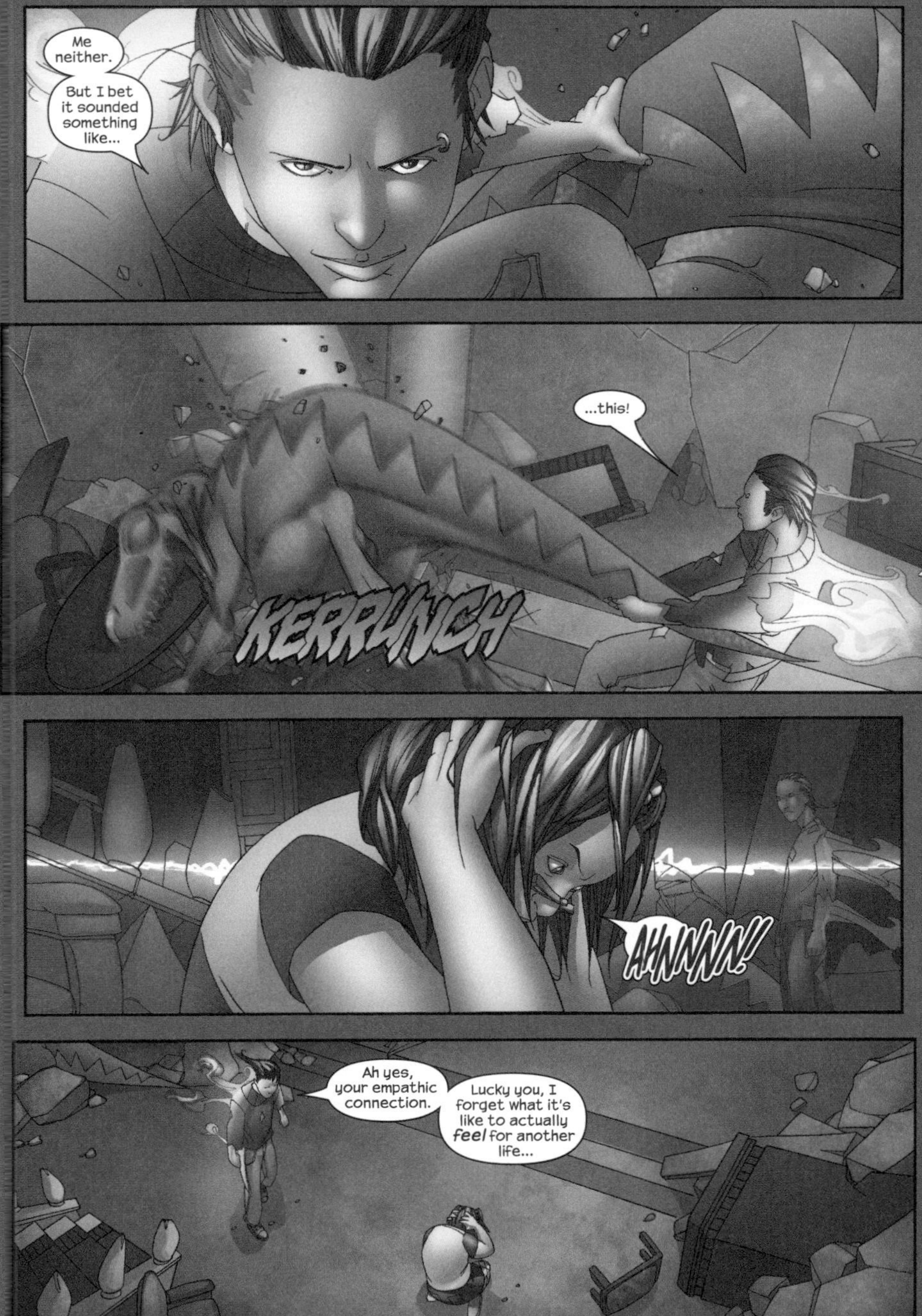
Me neither.
But I bet it sounded something like...
...this!
KERRUNCH
AHNNNN!!
Ah yes, your empathic connection.
Lucky you, I forget what it's like to actually *feel* for another life...

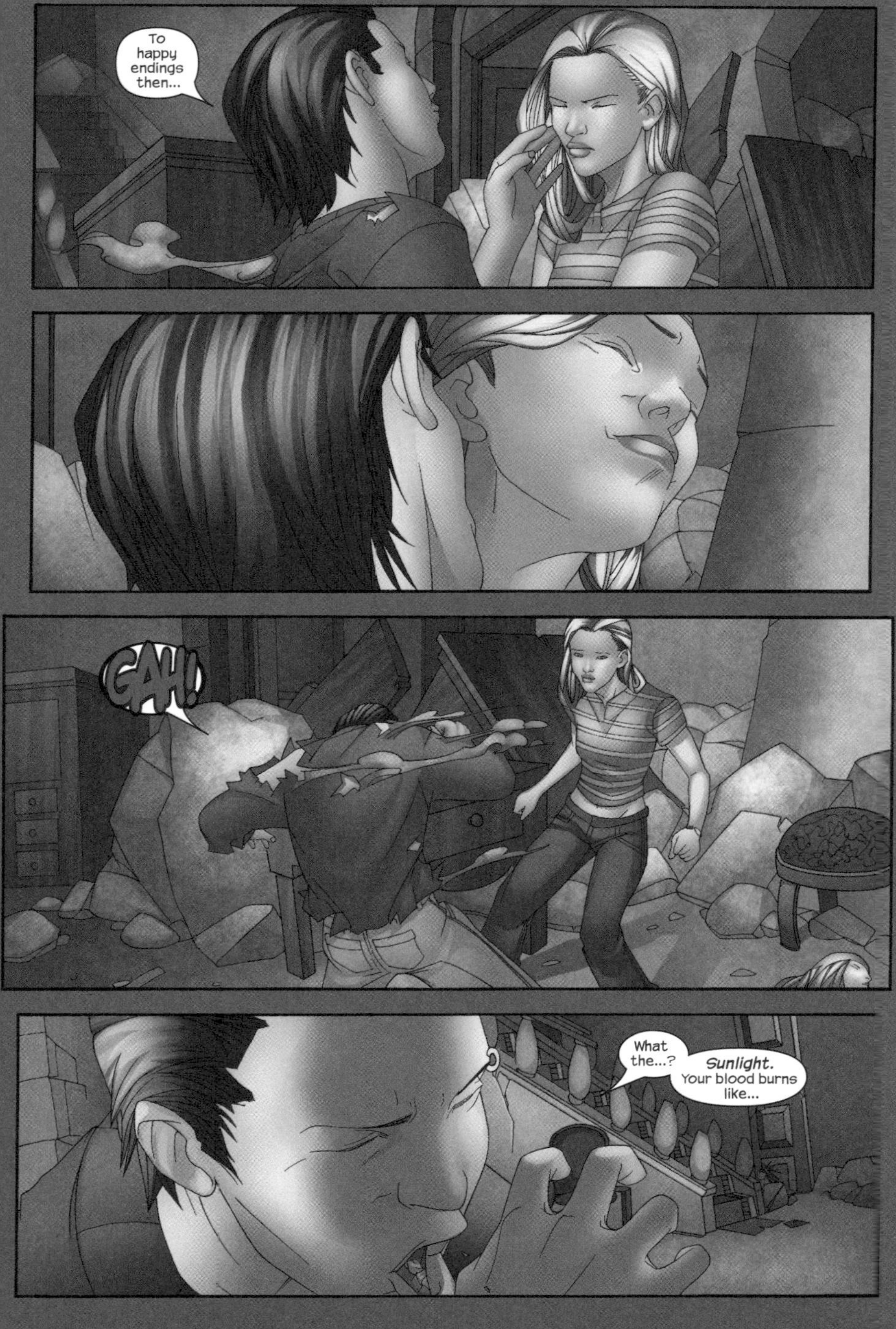
To happy endings then...
GAH!
What the...?
Sunlight. Your blood burns like...

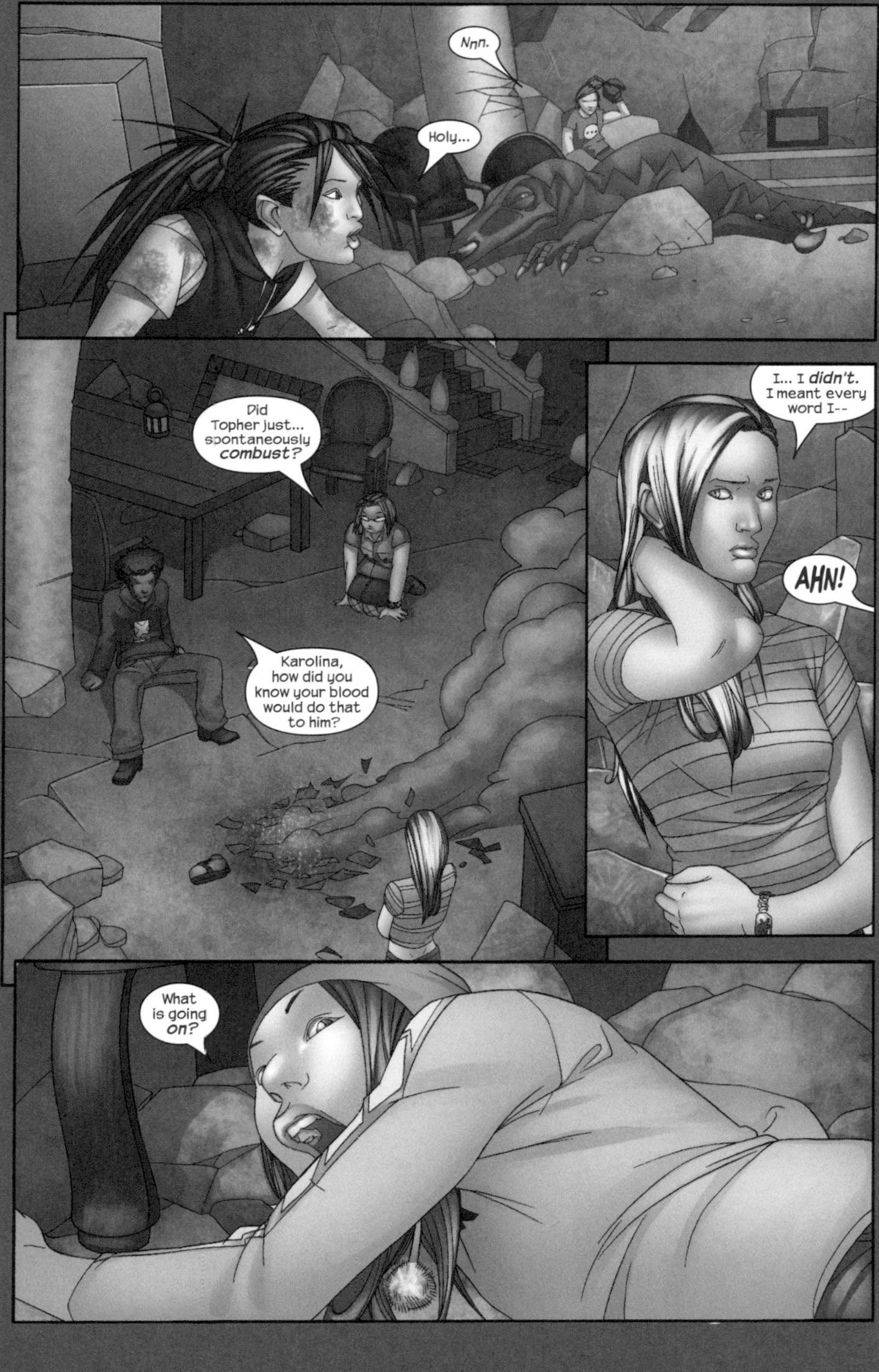
Nnn.
Holy...
Did Topher just... spontaneously *combust*?
Karolina, how did you know your blood would do that to him?
I... I *didn't.* I meant every word I--
AHN!
What is going *on*?

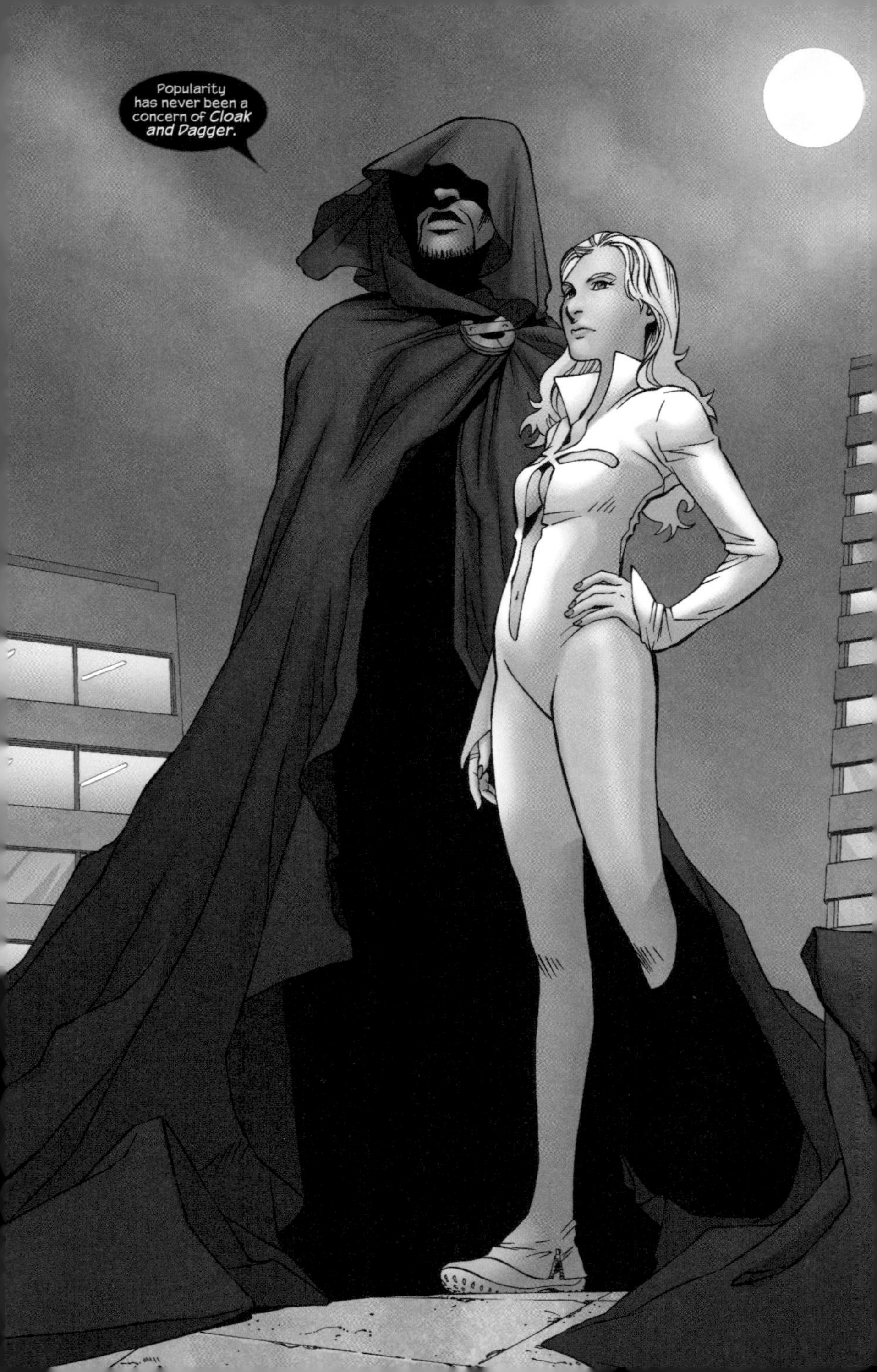
Popularity has never been a concern of *Cloak and Dagger*.

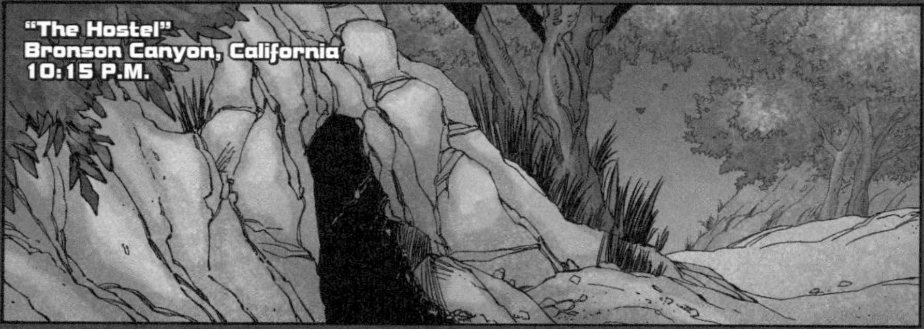
"The Hostel"
Bronson Canyon, California
10:15 P.M.

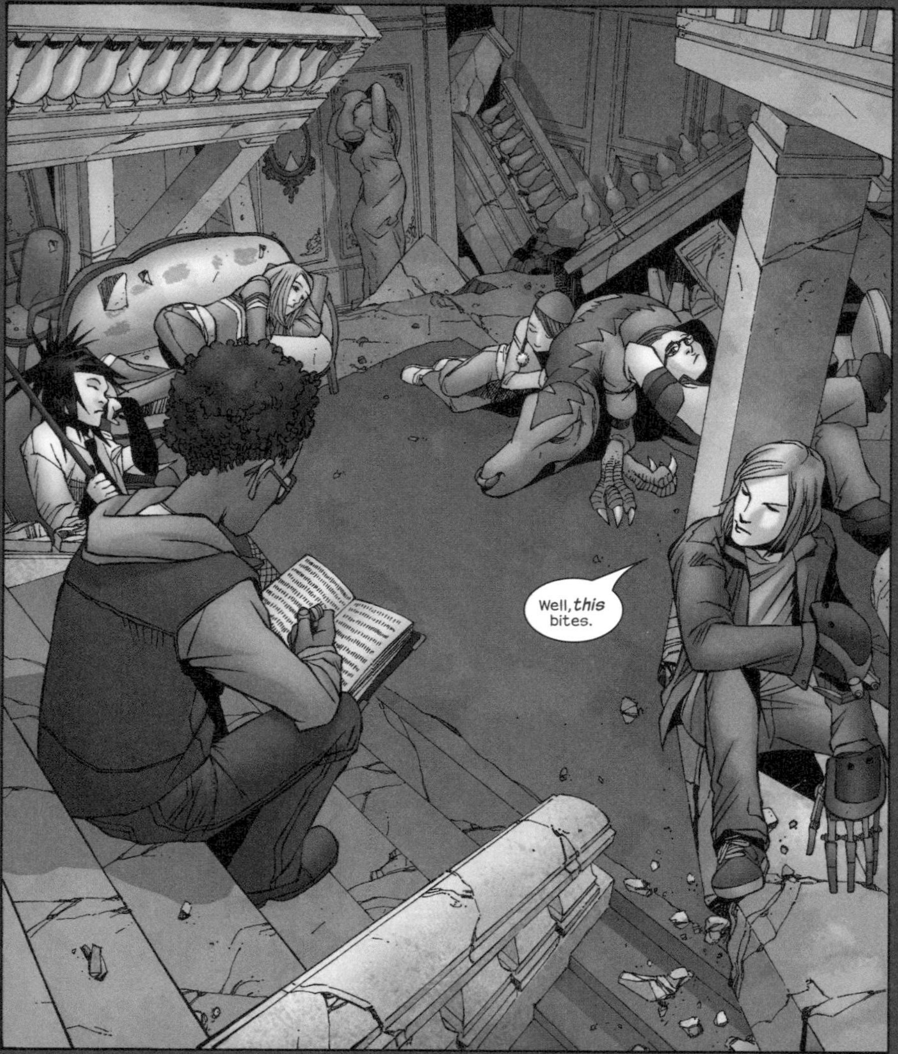
Well, *this* bites.

Well, you'll be pleased to know that it took my lovely wife and me all of two minutes to counterfeit the new fifty.

Not that The Pride will be strapped for cash anytime soon, after I used the Spine of Agamotto to install that musclebound *lummox* as our governor.

Enough with the back-patting, already! What of our *children*?

We have yet to receive another message from whichever of the runaways is our *mole*...

...but my husband and I have devised a *plan* if and when this mysterious asset helps us locate our progeny.

AHH!

OYE!

Leave now, or she'll be popping *spleens* instead of paint cans.

Nah, son, the only thing popping 'round here's gonna be a *cap* in your mutie--

What is this, a bad remake of West Side Story?

I hate when people mess with the *classics*.

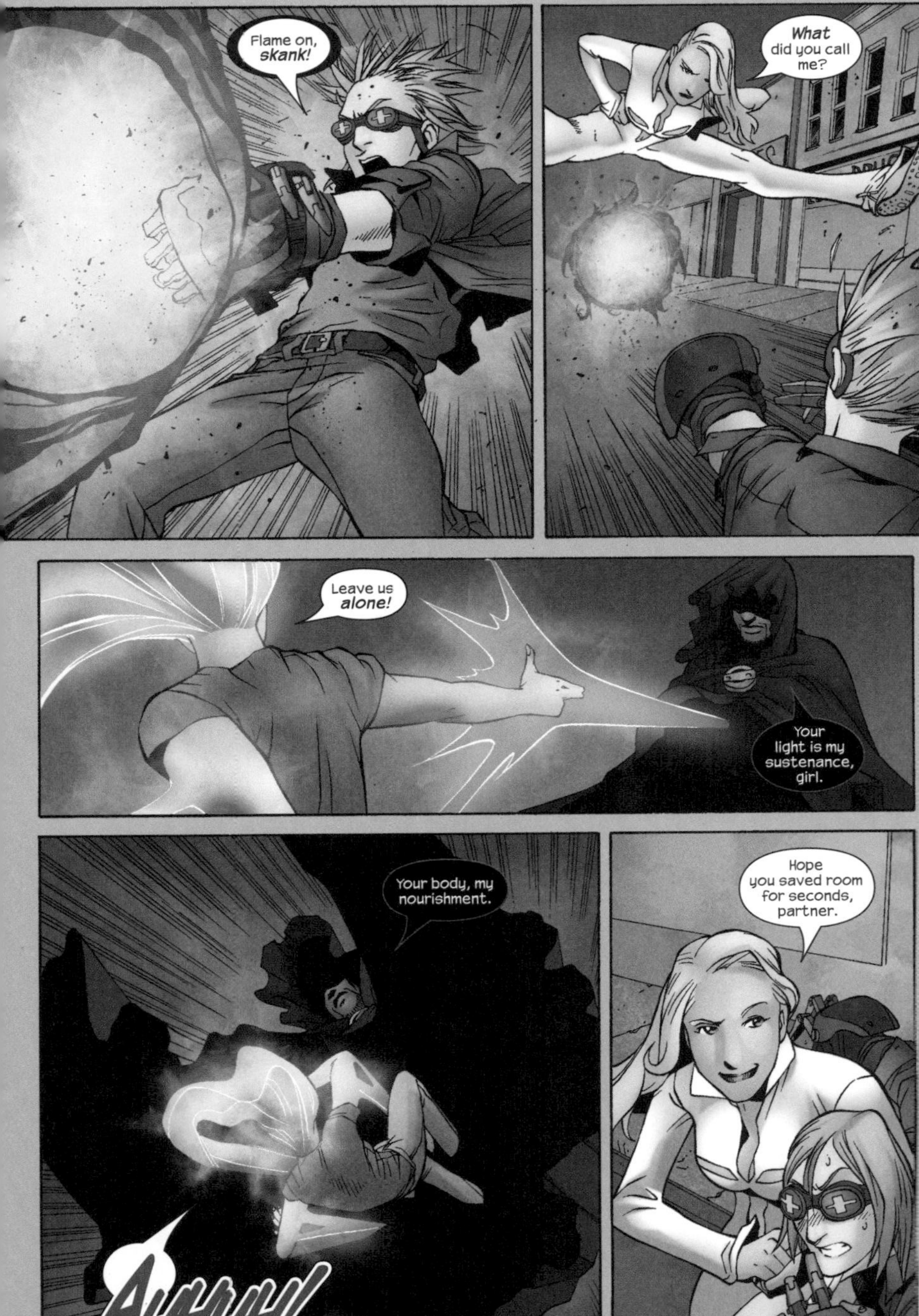
Flame on, skank!
What did you call me?
Leave us alone!
Your light is my sustenance, girl.
Your body, my nourishment.
AHHHH!
Hope you saved room for seconds, partner.

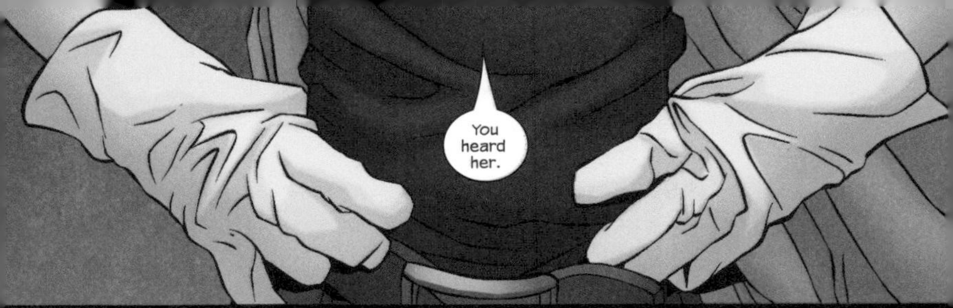
You heard her.

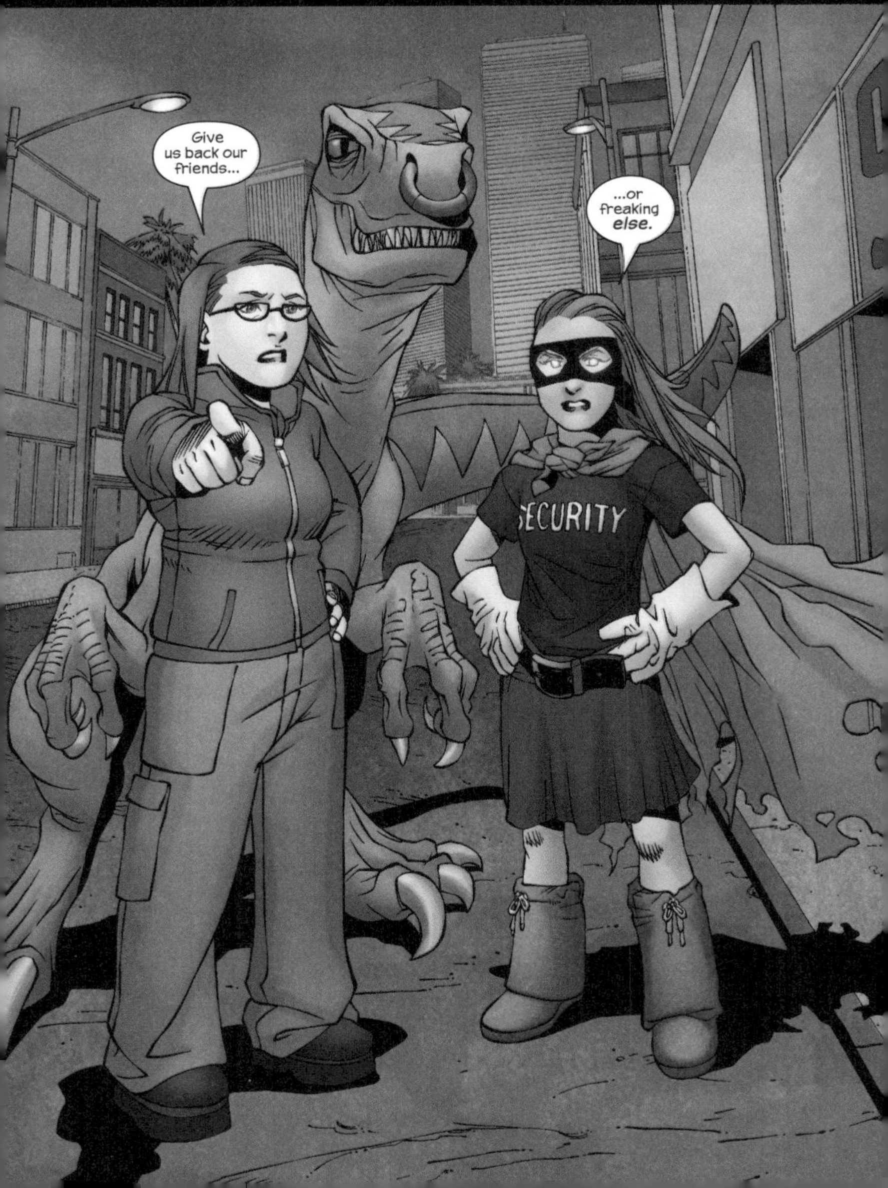
Give us back our friends...
...or freaking *else.*
SECURITY

12

Van Nuys, California
12:26 A.M.
Huh.
You know, it says a lot about my life that this *isn't* the strangest thing I've ever seen.

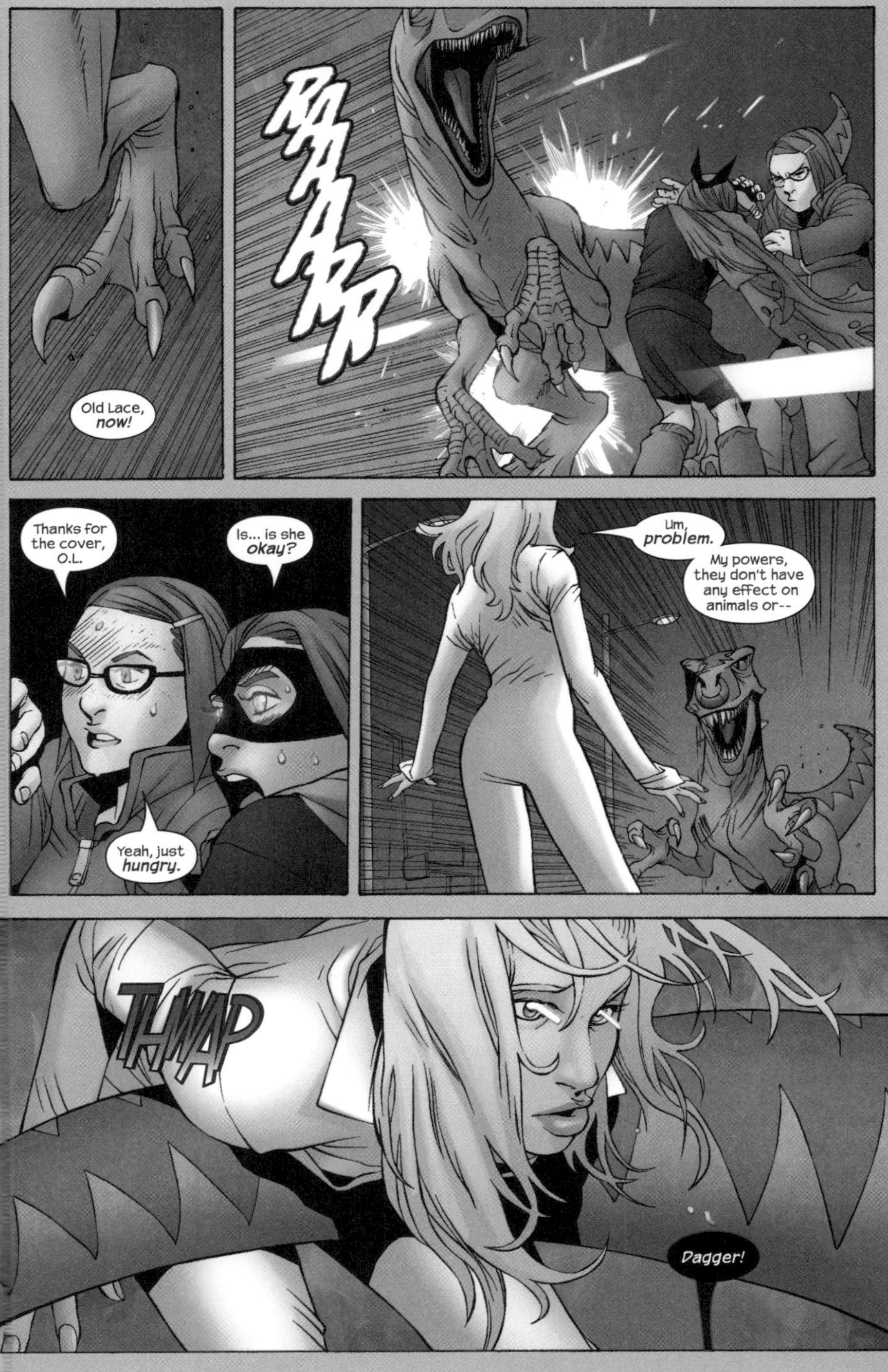

Old Lace, now!
RAAAARR
Thanks for the cover, O.L.
Is... is she okay?
Yeah, just hungry.
Um, problem.
My powers, they don't have any effect on animals or--
THWAP
Dagger!

Twenty-nine Minutes Later...

So this Lieutenant Flores jerk who put us on your scent...?

Yeah, sounds like he's an agent of The Pride, too. I'm sorry, they've got their fingers in *everything.*

We want our parents taken down *hard* for what they've done, but obviously, we're not quite Earth's Mightiest Heroes yet.

Speaking of which, I'm good friends with the Black Widow.

I'm sure she could put you in touch with Captain America and those guys, maybe send *them* out here to clean house.

Are... are you serious? That would be *amazing!*

In the meantime, you children are clearly not safe in Los Angeles. You will come back to New York with us.

In *that* thing?

No offense, bro, but I'd sooner spend the night at Neverland Ranch.

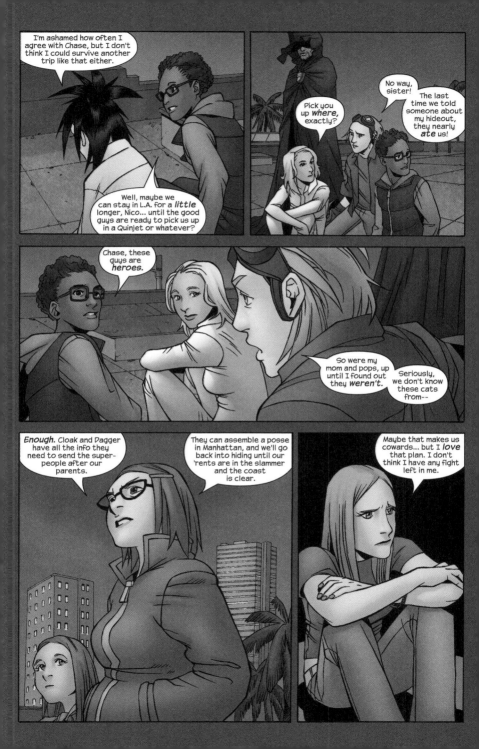

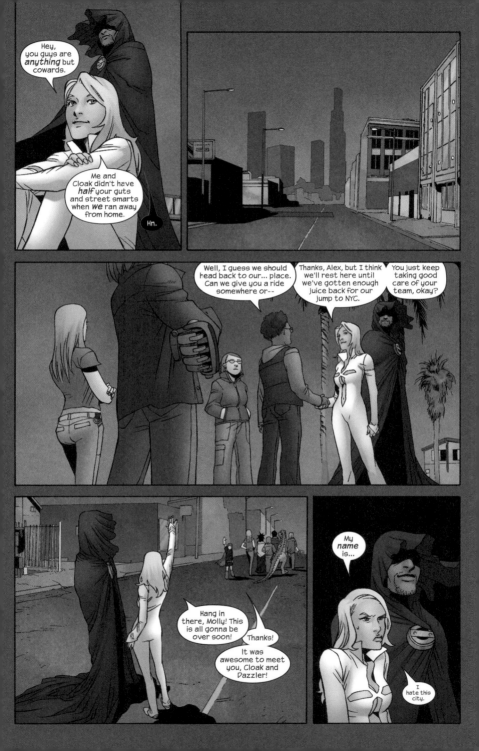

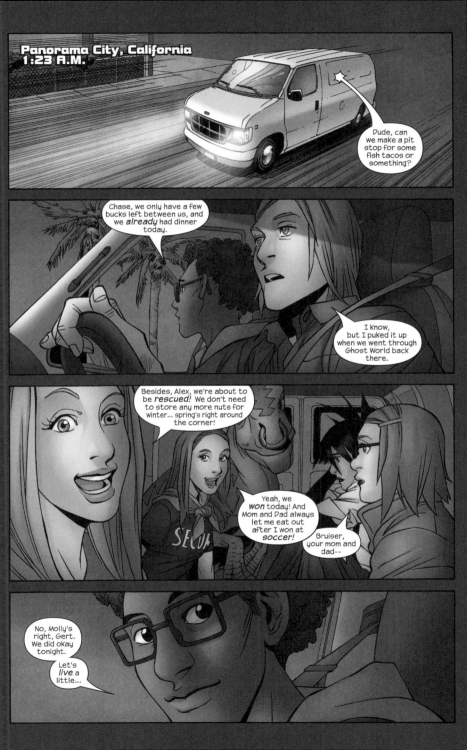

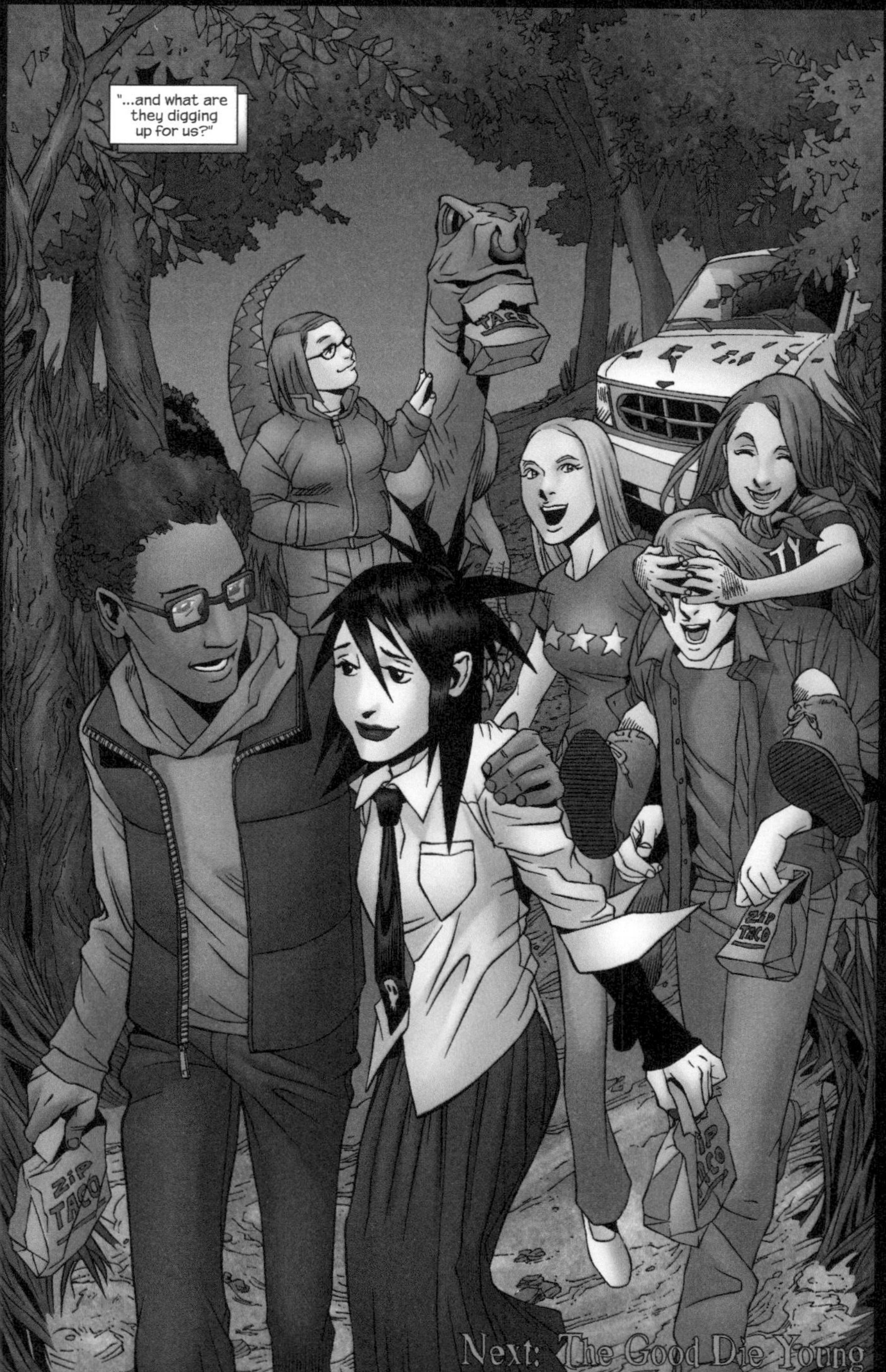
"...and what are they digging up for us?"
ZIP TACO
Next: The Good Die Young

PROMOTIONAL SKETCHES BY ADRIAN ALPHONA

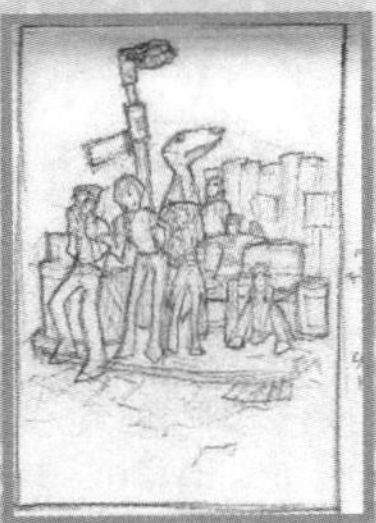

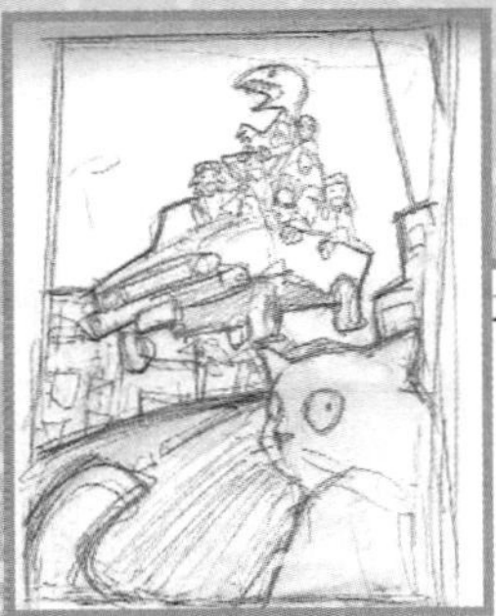

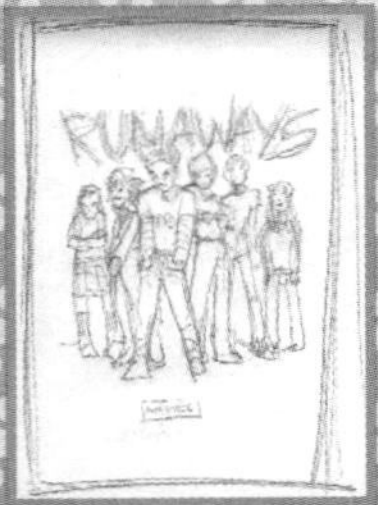
RUNAWAYS

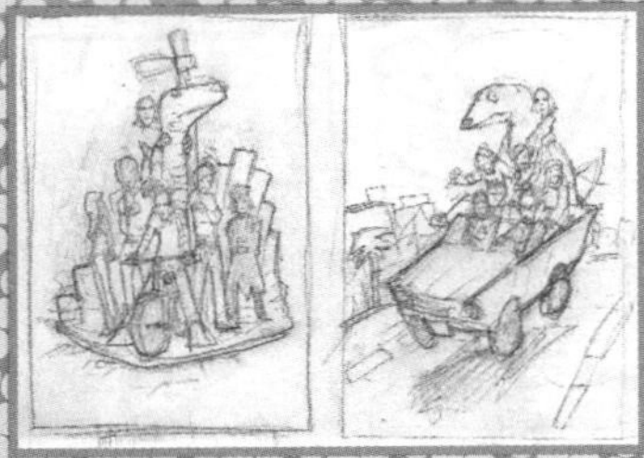

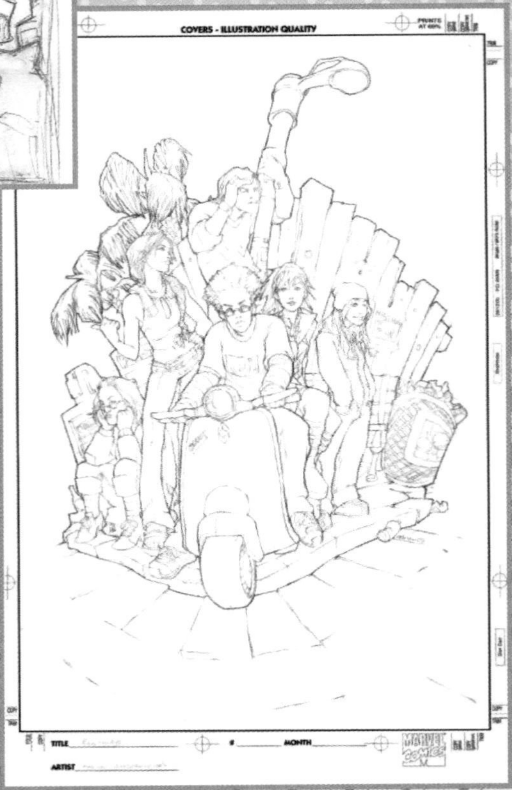
COVERS - ILLUSTRATION QUALITY
TITLE
MONTH
ARTIST
MARVEL COMICS

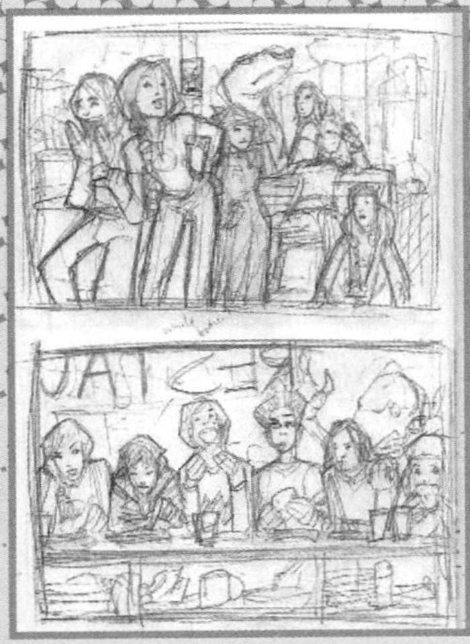

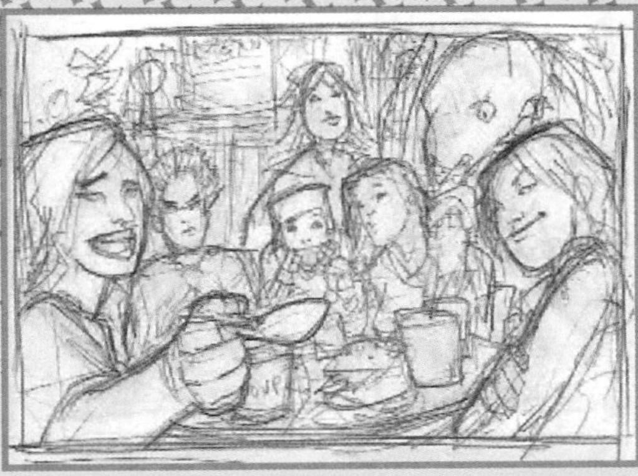

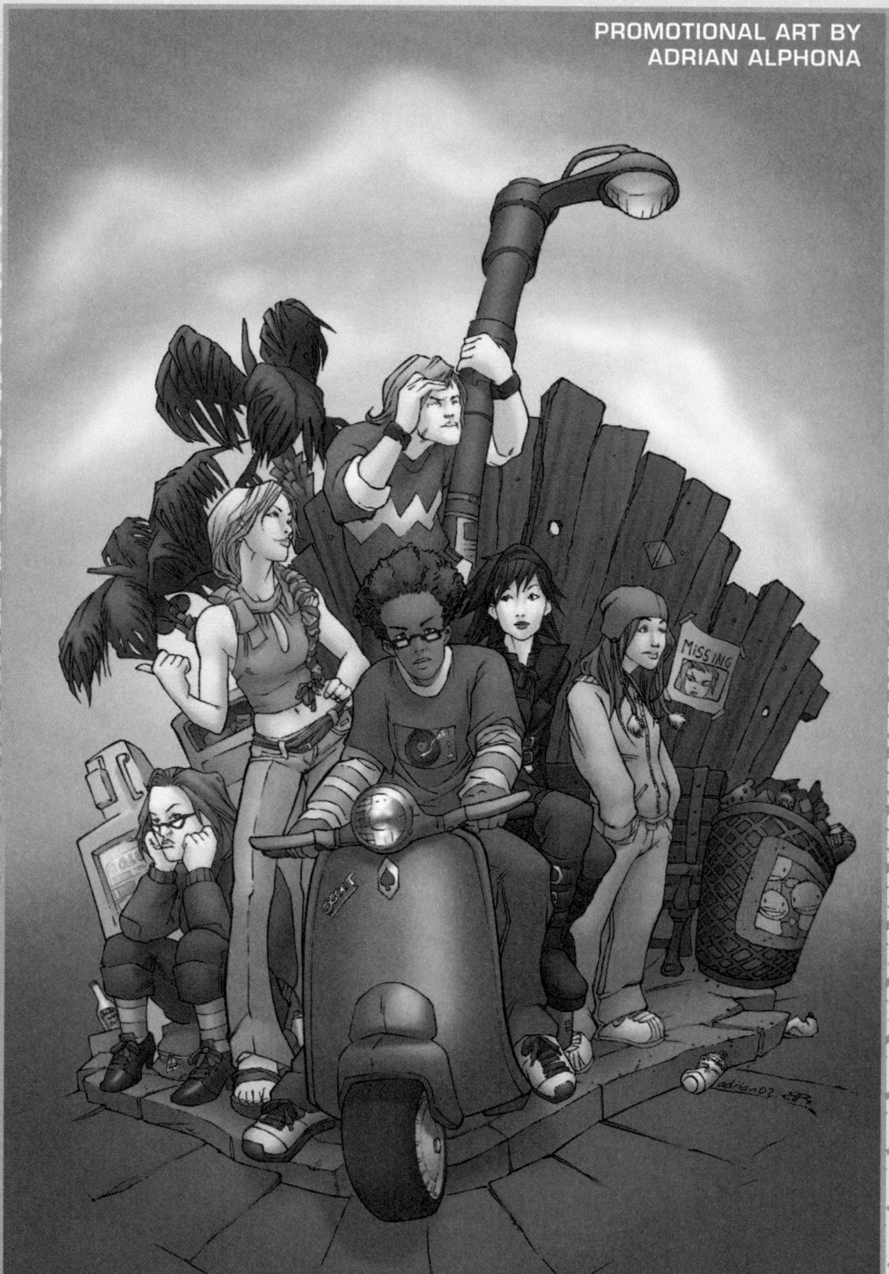
MISSING

PROMOTIONAL ART BY
ADRIAN ALPHONA

VOLUME 1 HARDCOVER ART BY
ADRIAN ALPHONA

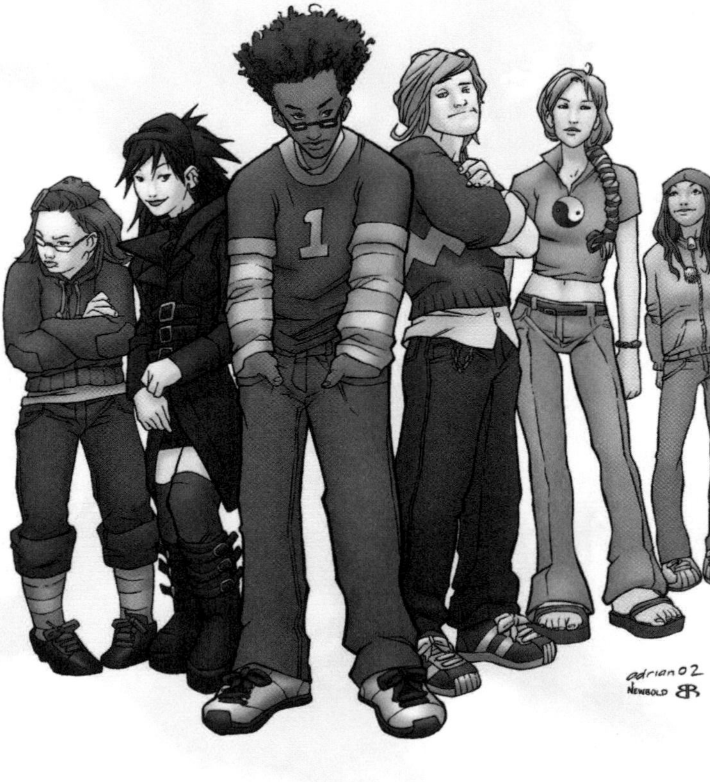
adrian 02
NEWBOLD

ADRIAN ALPHONA SKETCHBOOK

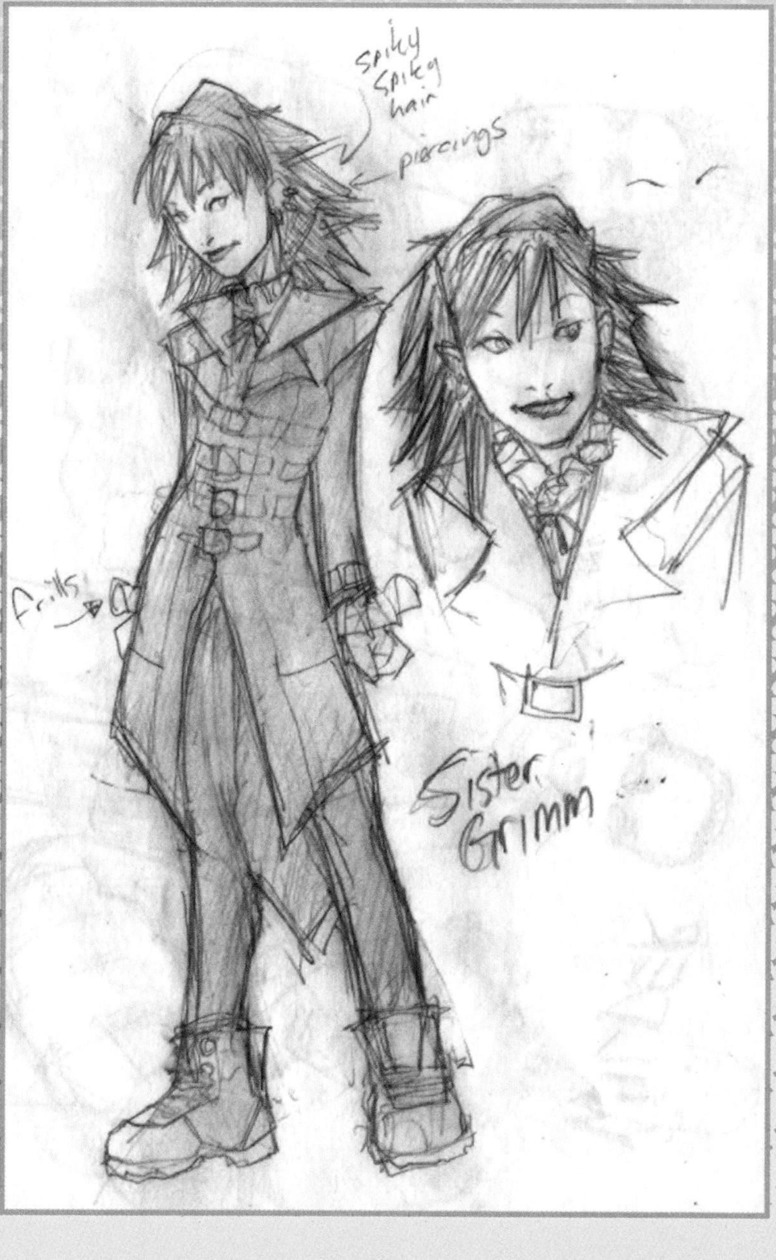
Spiky Spiky hair
piercings
Frills
Sister Grimm

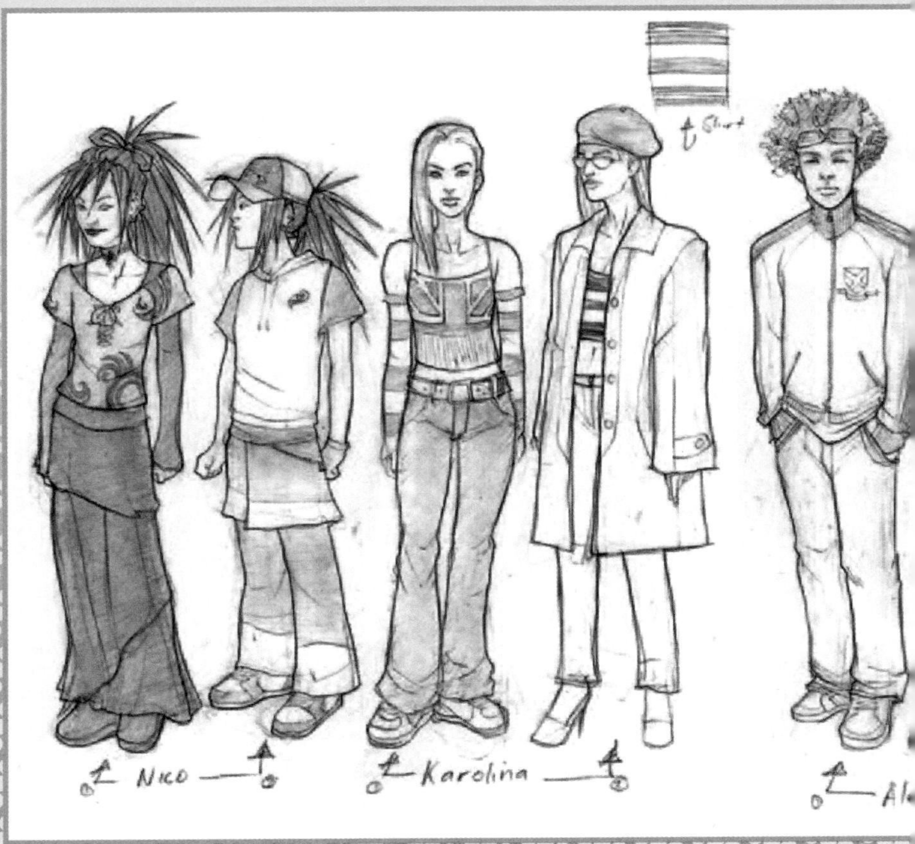
Shirt
Nico
Karolina

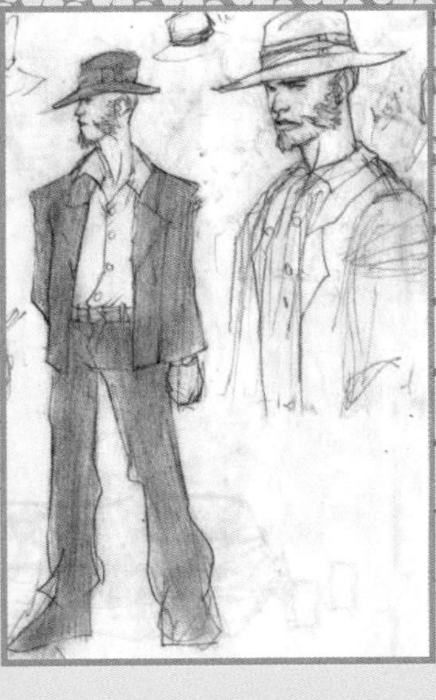

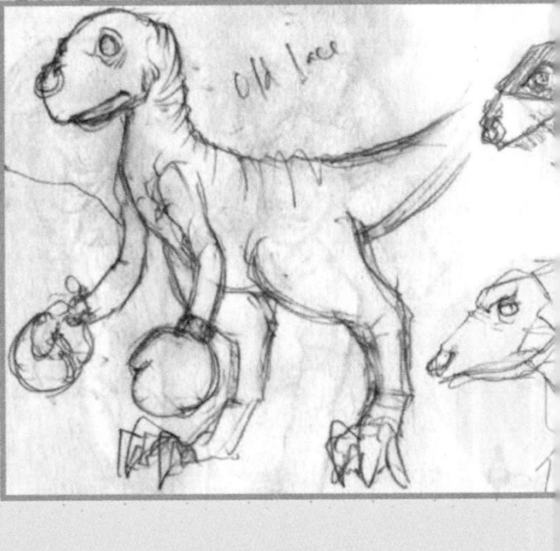
Old lace

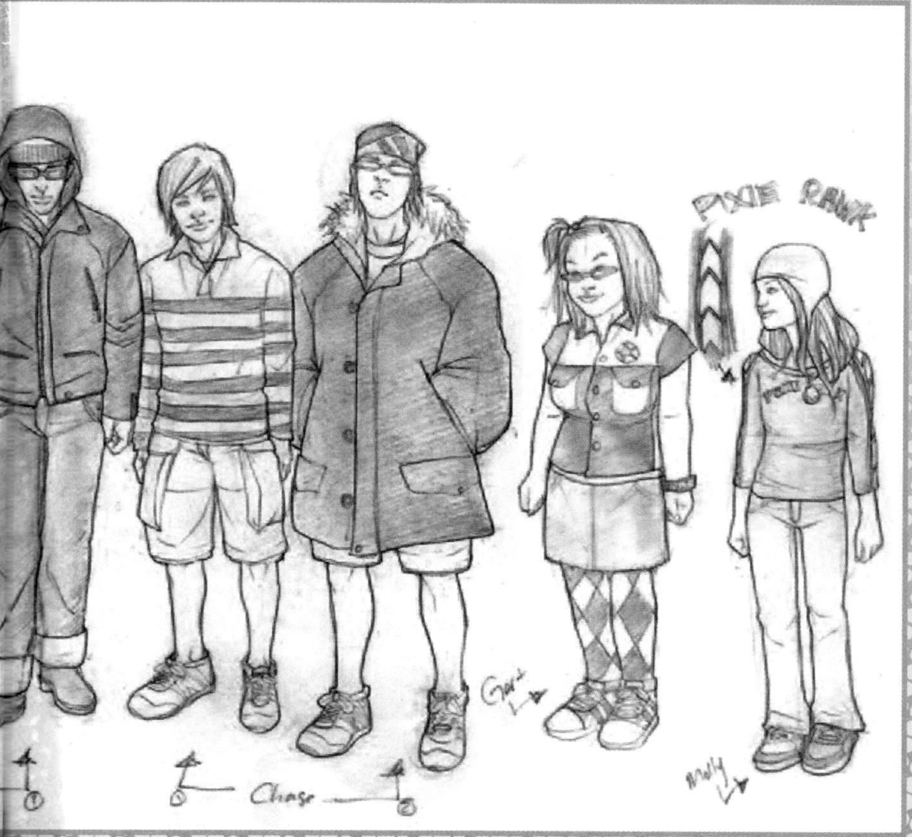
PIXIE RAWK
Chase
Gert
Molly

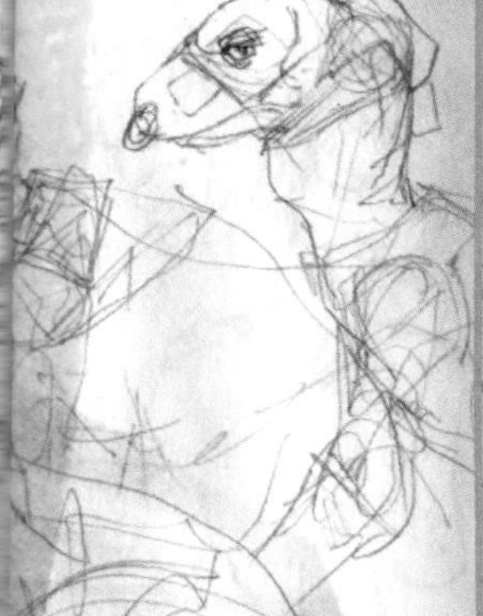

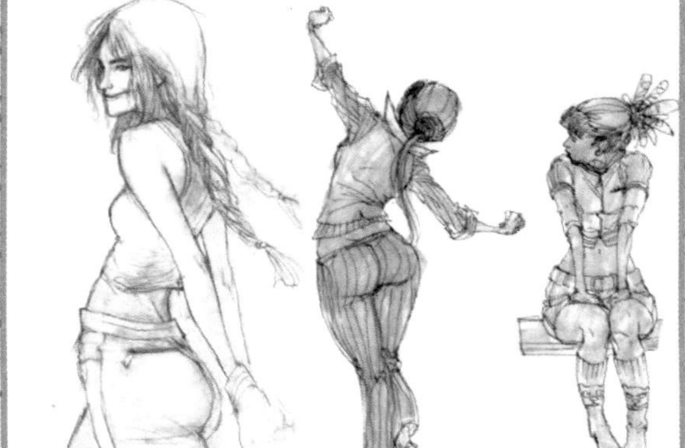

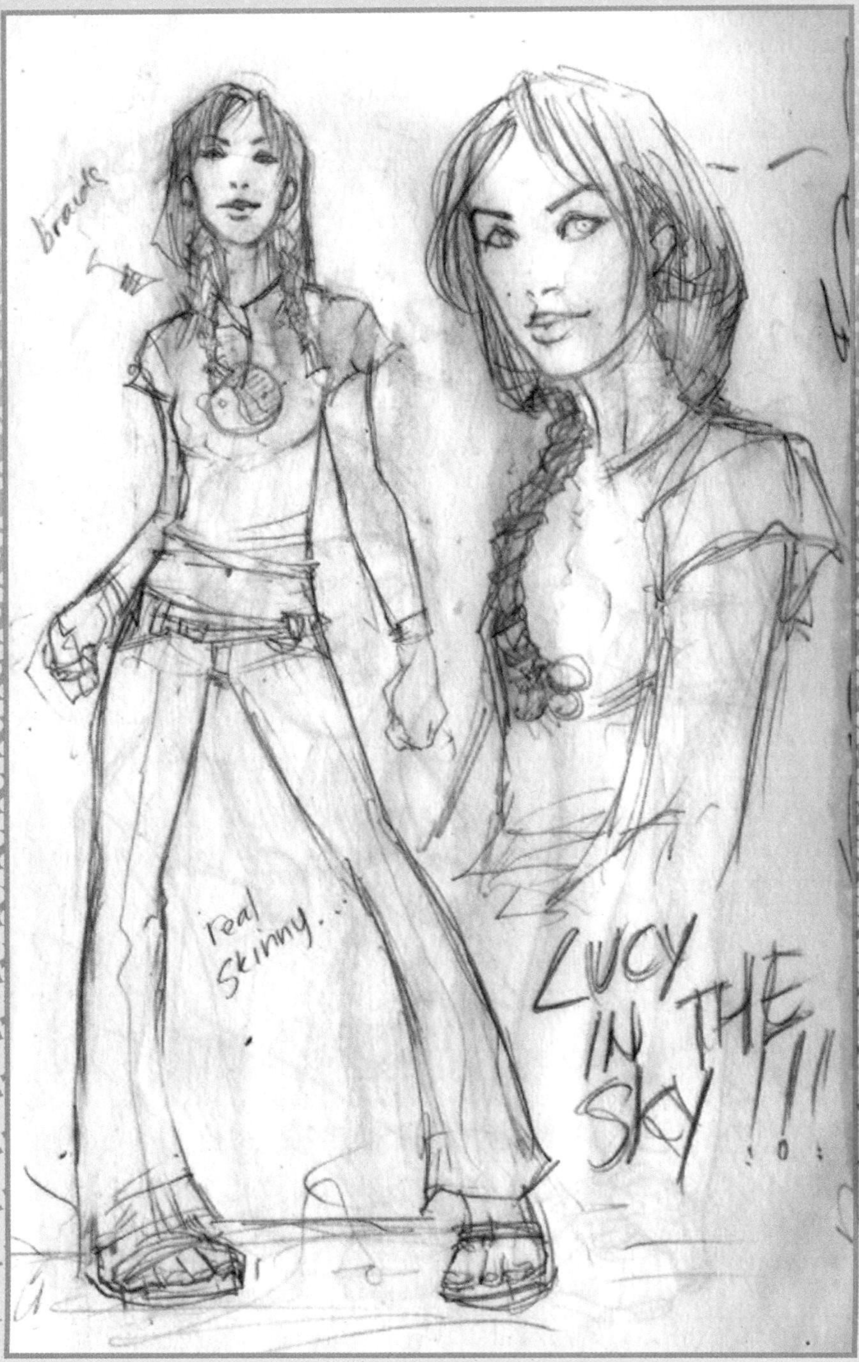
braids
real skinny.
LUCY IN THE SKY!!